D0412681
CANCELLED

Plan a Secure
Retirement

Trevor Goodbun

Teach®
Yourself

For UK order enquiries: please contact Bookpoint Ltd,
130 Milton Park, Abingdon, Oxon OX14 4SB.
Telephone: +44 (0) 1235 827720. Fax: +44 (0) 1235 400454.
Lines are open 09.00–17.00, Monday to Saturday, with a 24-hour
message answering service. Details about our titles and how to
order are available at www.teachyourself.com

Long renowned as the authoritative source for self-guided learning –
with more than 50 million copies sold worldwide – the **Teach Yourself**
series includes over 500 titles in the fields of languages, crafts, hobbies,
business, computing and education.

British Library Cataloguing in Publication Data: a catalogue record
for this title is available from the British Library.

This edition published 2010.

The **Teach Yourself** name is a registered trade mark of
Hodder Headline.

Copyright © 2010 Trevor Goodbun

In UK: All rights reserved. Apart from any permitted use under UK
copyright law, no part of this publication may be reproduced or
transmitted in any form or by any means, electronic or mechanical,
including photocopy, recording, or any information, storage and
retrieval system, without permission in writing from the publisher
or under licence from the Copyright Licensing Agency Limited.
Further details of such licences (for reprographic reproduction)
may be obtained from the Copyright Licensing Agency Limited,
of Saffron House, 6–10 Kirby Street, London EC1N 8TS.

Typeset by MPS Limited, A Macmillan Company.

Printed in Great Britain for Hodder Education, an Hachette UK
Company, 338 Euston Road, London NW1 3BH, by CPI Cox &
Wyman, Reading, Berkshire RG1 8EX.

The publisher has used its best endeavours to ensure that the URLs
for external websites referred to in this book are correct and active
at the time of going to press. However, the publisher and the
author have no responsibility for the websites and can make no
guarantee that a site will remain live or that the content will remain
relevant, decent or appropriate.

Hachette UK's policy is to use papers that are natural, renewable
and recyclable products and made from wood grown in sustainable
forests. The logging and manufacturing processes are expected to
conform to the environmental regulations of the country of origin.

Impression number   10 9 8 7 6 5 4 3 2 1

Year   2014 2013 2012 2011 2010

Front cover: © Andrew Paterson/Alamy

Back cover: © Jakub Semeniuk/iStockphoto.com, © Royalty-Free/Corbis,
© agencyby/iStockphoto.com, © Andy Cook/iStockphoto.com,
© Christopher Ewing/iStockphoto.com, © zebicho – Fotolia.com,
© Geoffrey Holman/iStockphoto.com, © Photodisc/Getty Images,
© James C. Pruitt/iStockphoto.com, © Mohamed Saber – Fotolia.com

Photo credits: pp. xxxiv, 46, 106, 210: © Stockbyte/Photolibrary Group Ltd;
p. 158: © malcolm romain/iStockphoto.com

DUNDEE CITY
COUNCIL

SCIENCE AND BUSINESS

COO 583 964X

SUPPLIER	PRICE
WAT	£10.99

CLASS No.	DATE
332.02401	25/2/11

Contents

Disclaimer

Every effort has been made to make all of the information contained in this book as complete and accurate as possible. However this book should be used only as a general guide and the use of information in this book is at the reader's own risk.

It is sold with the understanding that neither the author nor the publisher are rendering legal, financial, investment or other professional advice or services and any such questions relevant to those areas should be addressed to qualified members of those professions.

Meet the author

With 30 years' experience in advising others on planning for their retirement, I was one of the first advisers in the UK to be awarded the title of Chartered Financial Planner.

As well as advising clients in my own IFA Practice, I run retirement planning seminars to prospective clients and professional groups and have broadcast on BBC Radio Norfolk, providing expert advice on a wide range of money-related issues.

I also write and deliver training on retirement issues for other financial advisers, with my current focus being on running exam revision courses. The combination of both training others and advising helps me to combine the theoretical with the practical aspects of retirement advice, as well as keep me up to date.

Although I have an in-depth understanding of pensions, I firmly believe that a pension is a means to an end – not an end in itself – and I always use a range of solutions to ensure that my clients will be able to enjoy the retirement that they deserve.

I live in Norwich with my partner and two children and, like most parents, spend much of my spare time running the kids back and forth to rugby, hockey, ski clubs and scouts, and I must also confess to an interest in model railways.

Trevor Goodbun

Only got a minute?

What does retirement mean to you?

What does the word 'retirement' mean to you? For some it conjures up an image of having to watch every penny, for others a Caribbean cruise or achieving a lifetime's ambition. For most it will not mean either of these things, but what is true for many is that the traditional image of the pensioner is not one they recognize in themselves.

Increasingly, retirement is not a single event, when the world as you know it suddenly ends, but a change of lifestyle that will continue to change over the years. Even the word is open to question, with many over retirement age working not because they have to but because they want to.

This means that before thinking about money, the first stage in preparing your retirement finances is to ask yourself what retirement will mean to you.

How much money will you need?

This is an easy question to pose but is much more difficult to answer, especially if you haven't answered the previous question about what retirement means to you. Nonetheless, making some attempt to calculate your expenditure can go a very long way to reassuring you about the income you need and what to do with your money.

Understanding pensions

Pensions can be incredibly complex, often unnecessarily so. The good news is that there are really only three types of pension, and having a basic understanding of how each of these works can go a long way to helping you make the right choices when you retire.

Pension choices

Depending on the type of pension you have, you may be able to secure a higher income if you shop around when you come to take your pension. Yet six out of ten people who could be better off by doing this stay with their existing pension company and lose out on an increased income for the rest of their lives.

Investing in retirement

When you are retired you will often have two conflicting needs, one to create as much growth or income as possible from your savings, the other to preserve the capital you have built up over the years. Unfortunately there is no perfect answer to this, but more often than not it's possible to find a compromise that is right for you.

Tax and NI

A recent Audit Office report in 2009 found that 1.5 million pensioners have overpaid a total of £250 million in tax since 2002. Another 3.2 million did not claim all of the allowances they were entitled to.

There were a number of reasons for this, but the common thread was they did not realize and capitalize on the advantageous tax treatment that exists for those who are not working and/or are over the age of 65.

Getting advice

One of the dilemmas I had when writing this book was how to strike the balance between giving enough information to live up to the Teach Yourself title whilst conveying the intricacies of a subject that has taken me most of my working life to learn. Inevitably this means that I cannot cover every circumstance or give precise details for everything – you may need to seek professional advice to further your investigations. However, if you do need more advice then the contents of this book will at least point you in the right direction.

5 Only got five minutes?

Your five-minute jargon buster

One of the problems in dealing with any aspect of money is the jargon that is used. Whilst much of this can seem unnecessary, understanding the language can cut through the mist of confusion that can often surround the subject.

Age Allowance An additional amount of income you are allowed if you are over the age of 65 before you have to pay tax.

Annual Equivalent Rate (AER) The true rate of interest paid (usually on a deposit account) taking into account the rate of interest and how often the interest is paid. When comparing interest rates you should always compare the AER and not the headline rate.

Annuity An income, usually for life, that you buy with a lump sum. If you have a personal pension when you take the pension you will usually buy an annuity.

Asset class A way of describing the common characteristics of a particular type of investment. The main asset classes are: cash, fixed interest, property and equities. Most investments will fall into one of these asset classes.

Bond The most over-used word in financial services and one that seems to be used if no other description can be thought of. This means there can be no single definition, so whenever you see it make sure you investigate further to see what is actually on offer.

Cash One of the four main asset classes. As well as cash in your pocket it includes other items, such as Treasury Bonds.

Collective investment A way of joining with others to invest in a range of investments far wider than you could achieve on your own. Usually a professional fund manager will be appointed to manage the funds on a day-to-day basis. Open-Ended Investment Companies (OEIC) and Unit Trusts are examples of this type of investment.

Compulsory Purchase Annuity (CPA) An annuity bought with funds from a pension.

Contracting out If you are employed, instead of building up a second state pension you can contract out and build up a pension through your employer or a personal pension.

Coupon The interest paid on fixed interest investments. The coupon rate refers to the rate paid on the face value of the investment, not the effective interest rate based on the price you paid.

Defined benefit pension A pension where the amount of pension paid is based on your salary and the number of years you have been a member of the pension scheme. The pension scheme has to provide the benefits promised irrespective of cost. Final salary pensions are the most common example of this type of pension.

Defined contribution pension A pension where money is invested to build up a lump sum that is then used to buy a pension. The amount of pension you can buy will largely depend on how much money has been saved, how much it has grown and pension rates when you come to take benefits. A personal pension is a type of defined contribution pension.

Drawdown A way of drawing income directly from your pension without having to buy an annuity.

Equities More commonly called stocks and shares, although technically in the UK only shares are equities. One of the four main asset classes.

Fixed interest investments One of the four main asset classes. Fixed interest pay a fixed rate of interest based on the face value of the investment. They can usually be traded after they have been issued and you may pay more or less than the face value.

Fund A description of where money is actually invested, e.g. UK Equity will be invested in shares in the UK. Not to be confused with an investment wrapper or vehicle.

Gross income The amount of income you receive before tax has been deducted.

Guaranteed Minimum Pension (GMP) The amount of pension built up in a defined benefit pension through contracting out until April 1997. Since that date the contracting out benefits are included with other benefits and cannot be separately identified.

Investment bond An investment where you choose an investment fund that is then managed by a professional fund manager. It works in a similar way to a Unit Trust or OEIC but is treated differently for tax.

Investment Trust A company set up to invest in other companies. The value of the Investment Trust's shares may trade higher or lower then the value of the shares it owns.

Level pension A pension that stays at the same level throughout and does not increase.

Lifetime Allowance The amount of money that an individual can build up in pensions before the favourable tax treatment is removed. The limit applies to the individual, not the scheme, so all pensions are included. Until 2015 this will be £1.8 million so will only affect a very small number of people.

Liquidity An expression used to explain how easy it is to access your money, or buy or sell an investment. Cash will usually be highly liquid, property highly illiquid.

Money Purchase Pension An alternative name for a defined contribution pension. You save in order to build up a fund that is then used to buy a pension.

Net income The amount of income you receive after tax and other deductions. Knowing the net income you receive is far more important than knowing the gross income as this is the amount you have available to you.

Non-Protected Rights The amount of pension built up in a defined contribution pension through your contributions, or your employer's, as opposed to Protected Rights, which is built up through contracting out.

Normal Retirement Date (NRD) The date a pension scheme sets for when you are expected to take your pension. You may be able to take benefits before or after this date, but there may be a penalty for taking benefits early and no advantage in delaying.

Open-Ended Investment Company (OEIC) A type of collective investment where shares are issued every time a person invests and cancelled when a person withdraws their money.

The value of the shares directly relates to the value of the investments held. Apart from the legal structure they operate in the same way as a Unit Trust.

. . . .

Pension Commencement Lump Sum (PCLS) The amount of lump sum that can be paid when you take your pension. It used to be known as tax-free cash and in the vast majority of cases is still not subject to tax.

. . . .

Personal Allowance The amount of income you can have before you have to pay Income Tax. Everyone with an income of less than £150,000 a year has a Personal Allowance. If your income is greater than the Personal Allowance you only pay Income Tax on the amount over the Personal Allowance.

. . . .

Property One of the four main asset classes. When included in an investment it will tend to be commercial as opposed to residential property.

. . . .

Protected Rights The pension built up in a defined contribution pension scheme through contracting out. The key difference from Non-Protected Rights benefits is that if you are married or in a civil partnership you must take a spouse's pension.

. . . .

Provider The expression used throughout this book to indicate the company providing your pension, investment etc.

. . . .

Purchased Life Annuity (PLA) An annuity bought with your 'own' money, as opposed to an annuity purchased from a pension fund.

. . . .

Single-life pension A pension paid to one person, i.e. it will not continue when that person has died.

. . . .

Spouse's/dependants' pension A pension that will continue to be paid to a spouse or other dependant after the person originally taking the pension has died. The maximum age for a dependant child is usually age 23.

....

Top slicing The way of calculating if any higher rate tax has to be paid on an investment bond. The profit is divided by the number of years the bond has been in force and then added to your income. If the two added together take you into higher rate tax then you will probably have to pay some tax.

....

Underlying investment The term used to explain where money is actually invested as opposed to the investment wrapper. For example, if you invested in a Unit Trust investing in UK Equities, the Unit Trust is the wrapper and the UK Equity Fund is the underlying investment.

....

Unit Trust A type of collective investment where units are issued every time a person invests and cancelled when a person withdraws their money. The value of the units directly relates to the value of the investments held. Apart from the legal structure they operate in the same way as an OEIC.

....

10 Only got ten minutes?

What will retirement mean to you?

Retirement is changing. No longer does it mean leaving a job in order to spend the last years of your life doing very little other than waiting for the grim reaper. For the vast majority of people it is as much about beginnings as endings, representing up to a third of their life. So what does retirement look like in the twenty-first century?

There are as many answers to that question as there are people. For some it means increased leisure time to travel, pursue a hobby or do things they simply didn't have time to do when working. For others it doesn't mean the end to work but a career change or the opportunity to start a new business. For some it is nothing but an artificial date that will make no difference other than they can draw their pension and get a bus pass.

Pensions and stopping work

Retirement usually coincides with drawing your pension, but if retirement means different things to different people this is no longer a certainty.

The timing of drawing your pension is now legally governed by your age, rather than whether or not you are working. With a few minor exceptions, you can draw your pension between the ages of 55 and 75 and, generally speaking, the earlier you draw your pension the less you will receive.

You can work and draw your pension, or work and delay taking your pension in order to take a higher income when you do stop working. Before deciding whether or not to take your pension, you need to decide if you need the income. If the answer is no, then it may be worth delaying in order to obtain a larger income a little later.

The three stages of retirement

It is tempting to think of retirement as a single stage in our lives, but for most of us it is not. I tend to think of retirement falling into three stages, each of the stages merging into each other but characterized nonetheless by distinct features.

In stage one, early retirement, most of us will be fit and healthy, reasonably active and may still work in some shape or form or another.

Stage two, the middle years, conforms closest to the traditional view of retirement where we will still be reasonably healthy but beginning to slow down.

In stage three, the later years, we may need help or indeed full-time care.

These three stages will be defined more by the way we feel rather than an arbitrary age. However, our monetary needs for each of these three stages will probably be different, with stages one and three having higher costs than stage two. At the same time, in stage one we may still be able to generate an income from working, so we need to bear this in mind when structuring our finances.

Understanding pensions

Having a basic understanding of pensions can make an enormous difference in helping you to decide what you will do with the choices you have when you come to take the benefits.

The basics are not that difficult to understand and, despite all the variations on a theme, there are only really three different types:

- final salary type schemes
- money purchase schemes
- state pensions

FINAL SALARY PENSIONS

With a final salary type scheme, the amount of pension you will receive is linked to your salary and the number of years you have been a member of the scheme. Every year you are a member you will earn a fraction of your final salary as a pension. For example, if your scheme paid a 60th for each year, you were a member for 20 years and your final salary was £30,000, you would receive a pension of £15,000, i.e. 20 × 1/60 × £30,000.

If you used to be a member of a final salary scheme but have now left, your pension will be based on your leaving salary and the number of years you were a member of the scheme. In most cases the pension will be increased to allow for inflation between the date you left and the date you take your pension, but the amount of increase will depend on the type of scheme and the date you left.

All final salary schemes have a Normal Retirement Date (NRD) when the benefits promised will be paid. It will usually be possible to take benefits before this date, in which case the amount paid will be reduced, or delay taking benefits, in which case the amount paid *may* be increased.

Most final salary schemes will pay a proportion of your pension to your husband or wife if you die before them, and most will allow you to take a lump sum, but this will mean your pension is reduced.

In fact, whether or not to take the lump sum will tend to be the only choice you have in the way you take benefits from a final salary pension and most people do even if, from a purely financial point of view, it may not always be the best value.

There are variations on this type of scheme, such as average salary pensions where your pension will be based on your average salary whilst you were a member rather then your final salary.

A pension that is directly linked to your salary and the years you have been a member of the scheme is technically called a defined benefit pension.

MONEY PURCHASE PENSIONS

The second type of pension is called a money purchase or defined contribution scheme. Personal pensions are an example of this type of scheme although many company pension schemes also work in this way.

The best way of understanding a defined contribution pension is to think of it in two distinct parts:

▶ firstly, a savings plan to build up a lump sum (often known as a fund)
▶ secondly, that fund is then used to buy an income for life.

You can only take 25% of the money you have accumulated in the fund as a lump sum (if you have been a member of the scheme before 2006 you may be able to take more than 25%), the rest must be used to buy an income.

The amount of pension you will receive will largely depend on:

▶ how much is saved into the pension
▶ how much that money grows
▶ how much pension you can buy with your pension fund

When you come to take your pension you will have a number of other choices, including whether to take a lump sum or increased income.

You will also be able to choose between buying an annuity or drawing an income directly from the pension fund, but most people will buy an annuity. An annuity is simply an income that will be paid for life no matter how long you live.

The amount of income you will receive from an annuity for a given purchase price will depend on what options you select, the main ones being:

- ▶ whether the income stays the same throughout your lifetime or increases
- ▶ whether the income will continue to be paid to your spouse if you die before them (a spouse's pension).

A level annuity that doesn't pay a spouse's pension will pay the greatest amount; an increasing annuity that pays a spouse's pension will pay the least.

STATE PENSIONS

The third type of pension is the state pension, which in turn subdivides into two types: the basic state pension and an earnings-related pension.

Provided you have paid or been credited with National Insurance contributions for 30 years or more you will receive the full basic state pension. If you have less than 30 years your pension will be reduced proportionately.

Currently men can take their state pension from age 65 and women, depending on their date of birth, between 60 and 65.

The second type of state pension is earnings related. The most well known version is SERPS. This will pay a pension based on your earnings between an upper and lower limit. You will only receive benefit for the years you have been employed and had earnings between the two limits.

It is possible to contract out of the earnings-related state pension (but not the basic state pension) and for the years you are contracted out you will earn benefits in the pension scheme used for this purpose instead of the state scheme.

You have to take benefits from the basic and earnings-related state pensions at the same time but you can delay taking both in return for an increased pension for up to five years. Each year you delay taking your state pensions will mean they will increase by just over 10%.

Shopping around for a pension

With very few exceptions you have a legal right to move your pension from your existing pension provider to a different one.

If your pension is a final salary or any other form of defined benefit pension, it is unlikely that you will be able to obtain a better pension than the one offered by your existing pension scheme. If, however, you have a defined contribution pension, either in the form of a company pension or personal pension, you should always shop around to see if you can obtain an increased pension elsewhere.

The likelihood of achieving this is even higher if you smoke or have a medical condition. The type of medical condition need not be that serious and it has been estimated that four out of ten people would be able to obtain a higher pension on medical grounds.

The easiest way of checking if you might be better off taking your pension elsewhere is to ask your existing pension provider for a transfer pack and transfer value. This will include examples of the pension they are offering and a transfer value which is the amount you could use to buy a pension elsewhere.

The biggest challenge you will face is the sheer number of variations on a theme: a pension with or without a lump sum, a level or increasing pension, a pension with or without spouse's benefit could all be quoted.

The solution is to identify the one closest to your requirements and then compare it with what is on offer elsewhere by checking the Financial Services Authority's (FSA) annuity comparison table. The easiest way of finding these tables is to enter 'FSA pension annuity comparison' into an internet search engine. This will show you if you are likely to be able to obtain a higher pension elsewhere and whether or not it is worth exploring further.

Finally, just to encourage you to do this, at the time of writing the best pension annuity rate for a 65-year-old man in good health paid nearly 10% more a year than the tenth best. If that 65-year-old was in poor health the difference was over 50%. This difference just covers the best ten rates – your existing pension may not even be in the top ten. Furthermore, the difference is not just a one-off but an increase that will literally last a lifetime.

Tax and National Insurance

If a 60-year-old man had an income from working of £30,000 a year, he would take home £1,885.30 a month.

A couple over the age of 65 equally sharing an income of £30,000 a year would take home £2,314.34 a year a month. This extra £431.04 is due to tax and National Insurance.

If a basic rate taxpayer placed £50,000 a year in an investment that paid 5% a year interest, they would pay £7,433 in Income Tax. (If they were a higher rate taxpayer they would pay £14,249.)

If that same person placed £50,000 a year in an investment that also grew at 5% a year, but was subject to Capital Gains Tax, they would only pay £5,660.01. With some simple, totally legal planning, they may avoid having to pay any tax at all.

A 65-year-old man earning £25,000 a year would take home £209.53 a month more than a 64-year-old because he would pay less tax and no National Insurance.

Tax may be boring and seem too difficult to try to understand, but as you can see a basic understanding can make a big difference to your standard of living.

Note: these figures are based on the tax year 2009/10 but unless there is a radical change in the tax system the fundamental principles will remain true.

Income Tax

Every UK resident with an income of less than £150,000 a year can have an income of a certain amount before they pay Income Tax. This is known as the Personal Allowance. In the tax year 2009/10 it was £6,475, although this amount is reduced for those incomes over £100,000 a year.

If your income exceeds your Personal Allowance you only pay tax on income over that allowance. The rate of tax is levied in bands and you pay tax at the rate applicable to the band. For example, if someone had an income of £25,000 they would pay tax as follows:

Income	Tax band	Rate	Tax to pay
First £6,475	Personal Allowance	Nil	Nil
Next £18,525	Basic rate	20%	£3,705
Total tax			**£3,705**

If they had an income of £50,000 their tax bill would be:

Income	Tax band	Rate (2009/10)	Tax to pay
First £6,475	Personal Allowance	Nil	Nil
Next £37,500	Basic rate	20%	£7,500
Next £6,025	Higher rate	40%	£2,410
Total tax			**£9,910**

One common misunderstanding of the UK tax system is that if you fall into another tax bracket the amount of income you will receive after tax will be reduced. Although the greater your income the higher percentage you will pay in tax, your net income can never reduce.

If you are over the age of 65 (the age limit of 65 applies to men and women) an additional allowance known as the Age Allowance means you are allowed more income before you pay tax, although if your income is over a certain level this additional allowance is gradually reduced until the Personal Allowance level is reached.

The Age Allowance means that if a couple over the age of 65 can split their income equally between them, they can have an income of £18,980 without paying a penny in Income Tax.

Income Tax is usually deducted at source which means tax is taken by the organization paying the income. Tax on savings interest is deducted at basic rate. If you are a higher rate taxpayer you will have to pay the difference between basic rate and higher rate.

If you don't pay any tax, you will not usually be able to reclaim the tax paid. This varies from product to product, although on deposit accounts you can ask for any interest to be paid without deduction of tax by completing a form known as a R85 which can be obtained from the product provider.

Capital Gains Tax

Often thought of as a 'rich man's tax', Capital Gains Tax is the biggest open secret when it comes to saving tax for the following reasons:

- ▶ it is charged at a lower rate than basic rate Income Tax
- ▶ there is only one rate so if you are a higher rate income taxpayer the tax saving is significant

- ▶ UK residents have a Capital Gains Tax allowance in addition to their Income Tax allowance and very few people use this allowance
- ▶ it is often relatively easy to move investments around to use the Capital Gains Tax allowance every year.

Capital Gains Tax is charged on any capital gain an investment makes as opposed to the income it generates. Usually it is easy to identify the difference between the two. For example, dividends from shares are income and are subject to Income Tax, whereas the increase in the value of the share is a capital gain and may be subject to Capital Gains Tax.

A gain is the profit that is made when an investment is disposed of; usually this will be when it is sold but can include other circumstances such as giving it away. The amount of the gain is usually the difference between the price paid and the sale price, less the cost of buying, selling and maintaining the investment.

In some circumstances the market price is used rather than the sale price in order to determine the gain and this is the valuation that would be used if you gave away an asset or sold at less than the market value.

As well as a Personal Allowance for Income Tax you have an Annual Allowance for Capital Gains Tax. In the tax year 2009/10 this was £10,100. This allowance applies to all gains on investments sold or disposed of in the year. Therefore, if you sold two or more investments you would only have one allowance, although of course if the gain from both was less than the allowance you wouldn't have any tax to pay.

Depending on the type of investment, it can sometimes be easy to sell it and buy another in order to use the Capital Gains Tax allowance every year. Obviously this isn't so easy if the investment is a buy-to-let property, but very easy to do with shares and many other types of investment. You have to wait 28 days before buying back the *same* investment for it to count as a disposal but there is nothing to stop you, say, selling BP shares and buying Shell instead, in which case you could use your Annual Allowance.

National Insurance

National Insurance is a tax by any other name which is charged on income from employment and self-employment.

The important point about this tax for readers of this book is that it is not paid on income from savings, investments and pensions, nor is it payable by anyone over state retirement age on any income.

What this means is that you need less gross income when you are retired in order to have the same net income as when you are working. If you combine this with the additional Income Tax Age Allowance this can be a significant difference.

Tax returns and forms

When you retire you will almost certainly start receiving forms from the tax office. It is worth taking time to complete these forms as accurately as possible to avoid paying any more tax than you need to. The main reason this can occur is that when you are retired you are more likely to have multiple sources of income and, unless the correct tax code is applied, too much tax may be deducted.

In fact, an Audit Office report in 2009 estimated that 1.5 million people over state retirement age overpaid tax by an average of £171 each, and a further 3.2 million did not fully claim their age related allowances.

Investments

The word 'savings' is usually used to describe regular saving into a low-risk product such as a deposit account. The word 'investing' is used to describe a lump sum being put into a riskier area such as shares, but this doesn't cover all circumstances. For example, is buying shares on a monthly basis saving or investing? And where does low risk stop and high risk start?

The key is not to worry about the language used, whether you are putting money away on a regular basis or as a lump sum. Whether that money is placed in a high-risk or a low-risk investment, the basic principles are the same.

Another issue is not to confuse the investment type and the investment itself. For instance, many perceive pensions to be risky and deposit accounts to be safe, but a pension is only an example of an investment wrapper and it is possible to invest in a deposit account through a pension. The word used for the investment type is 'investment wrapper' or 'investment vehicle'.

The secret with saving and investing is:

▶ firstly decide what you want or need
▶ then decide on the saving or investment most likely to meet that need
▶ only then choose the investment wrapper.

Too many people approach (or are often sold!) this the other way round, dismissing Unit Trusts and similar investments as being too risky when it is the actual investment that is placed in the investment wrapper that carries the risk and not the wrapper itself.

DECIDING WHAT YOU NEED

Before even thinking about where to save or invest your money, ask yourself what you want from it.

- ▶ Do you need income, growth or both?
- ▶ How long are you saving or investing for?
- ▶ Will you need access to your money at short notice?
- ▶ How much could you afford to lose assuming you kept the investment for the intended time?
- ▶ How much fall in value could you tolerate before you started losing sleep?

There are no perfect answers to these questions and nearly always a compromise has to be made. A deposit account may be relatively safe but may not generate the income you need. On the other hand, an investment that produces the income you need may involve a risk to your capital.

More than anything else, be very wary of anyone who tries to recommend the perfect solution because it just doesn't exist – or at least after 32 years I have yet to find it despite looking very hard!

DECIDING ON THE INVESTMENT

If you need instant access to your money, only want the lowest level of risk or will access your money within a relatively short time, say five years, then you really only have one choice which is a deposit account or similar investment.

Once you go beyond this, things get more complex, but there is a wide choice available covering most requirements.

DECIDING ON THE INVESTMENT WRAPPER

Only when you have decided what type of investment will meet your needs should you decide on the investment wrapper.

It is hard to disagree that everyone should use their ISA allowance but once this has been used there are a number of choices. The most suitable investment wrapper will largely be determined by which one will result in you paying the least tax, but other factors can also come into play.

Equity release

Equity release is a method of using the capital built up in your home in order to release capital or generate an income.

When they were first introduced, many equity release products turned out to be a very poor buy. In some extreme cases people ended up paying more in interest than the income they received and ended their lives owing more than the value of their home. This resulted in a bad reputation that has lingered to this day.

However, today's products bear no resemblance to those early products and sales are regulated: anyone who advises on them has to be specifically qualified and authorized to do so. They should also not be confused with lease-back schemes where you sell your house and then pay rent.

With a reputable equity release product:

▶ you can never owe more than your house is worth
▶ you do not pay rent or interest until you die or permanently move into care (in the case of a joint plan this is on the death etc. of the second person).

There are two main types of equity release plan:

▶ where you sell all or part of your home in return for a lump sum
▶ where you mortgage your home.

Plans where you sell your home are known as Home Reversion Plans and the company providing the plan will provide you with a capital sum in return for complete or partial ownership.

The provider will then benefit from the increase in value of the home in direct proportion to the amount they own. For example, if you sell 50%, the equity release provider will receive 50% of the proceeds when the house is sold following your death or when you permanently move into care, and you or your estate will receive the other 50%.

The other type of equity release is known as a lifetime mortgage. Unlike most other mortgages, with a Lifetime Mortgage you do not make any interest or capital payments while you remain in your home. Instead the interest is 'rolled up' and repaid as a single amount along with the capital when you die or move into care.

There are various types of Lifetime Mortgage available. Some will pay you an income, others will release a lump sum.

Because the longer the interest 'rolls up' the greater the amount that has to be repaid, the economics of equity release don't really stack up for most people until they are about 70 or 75 years old, so it is not really suitable for most people when they first retire.

That being said, when you first retire it is worth thinking about whether it may be an option later in life. The reason for this is that knowing you may be prepared to release capital from your home may influence the decisions you take initially. For instance, you may be prepared to take a pension that starts at a higher level but will be eroded by inflation, or to take a slightly higher investment risk in the knowledge that if the value of your investments fall you have a back-up.

Getting advice

It is impossible in a single book to cover every aspect of financial planning in retirement, partly because of the complexities involved and partly because everyone will have different requirements.

As a result it may be that you decide to seek professional advice, in which case reading this book will at least have prepared you to look for the right thing, ask the right questions and understand the answers.

The main area where advice may be required is finding the specific product or solution for your individual needs. This may include shopping around for the best pension rates, deciding on a specific investment or advice if you are considering equity release.

There are thousands of highly qualified, competent and honest advisers out there – it is finding them that is the issue. There are listings of advisers and you only have to mention the fact you are looking for financial advice to your bank and they will almost jump over the counter to embrace you!

The following may help you find an adviser:

- ▶ Use an Independent Financial Adviser. They are not tied to one company and are legally obliged to act for you. You can find an adviser near you by visiting www.unbiased.co.uk or look in the *Yellow Pages*.
- ▶ Shop around and ask several different advisers what they can offer, but be wary of anyone who offers a perfect solution.
- ▶ Ask the adviser for their qualifications and experience, specifically in dealing with the area where you want help.
- ▶ Ask the adviser if you can talk to other clients about what they have done for them.
- ▶ Ask to see examples of reports they may have written covering similar circumstances to yours.
- ▶ Expect the adviser to be open and honest about what they charge. Very few things in life are free and good financial advice is rarely one of them. If they say they will be paid by commission you need to realize this is not free, it is just a different way of paying.

1

What do you want from retirement?

In this chapter you will:
- *think about what retirement means to you*
- *learn about the three stages of retirement*
- *consider the choices facing you when you retire*

What do you mean by retirement?

Insight

Most of us have a concept of retirement that is in many
ways outdated. This view is one that has been shaped by our
parents or even grandparents, where a person works hard all
of their lives, reaches an arbitrary age, retires and often dies
shortly afterwards. The reality is that for the vast majority of
people, retirement will be very different from this. Most will
still be in good health, many will want to continue working
and many will use retirement as the opportunity to achieve
a long-held ambition. In fact, retirement usually means
replacing one activity with a series of others.

The fact you are reading this book presumably means you are
giving at least some thought to retirement. But what do you
mean by retirement? Do you mean stopping work? Do you mean
drawing your pension? Do you mean both of these things or
something completely different?

Things used to be clear cut. As a man you would work until 65, a woman until 60, then retire, draw your pension and often die a few years later. Alternatively, about 20 years ago many people 'retired' at 50, although in many cases this was redundancy by a different name. The lucky ones had an attractive inflation protected final salary pension and could spend many years at leisure. For those who were not so lucky, retirement really meant a severely reduced income with little or no opportunity to find work again.

The reality today is that the lines between work and retirement have become blurred, and instead of the stark distinction between work and retirement there are multiple shades of grey. This could mean leaving one job for another, working part time or even undertaking voluntary work.

Even if retirement means you stopping paid work altogether, the probability is that you will not recognize the mainstream, even comedic view of a 'pensioner'. Hopefully you will still be in good health, you may have plans to travel or achieve a long-held ambition, or just do some of the things you didn't have time to do when working.

Pensions and stopping work

Insight

Whilst we usually link drawing our pension with stopping work, the two can be unrelated, with many pensions having a great deal of flexibility about how and when we draw benefits.

The law says that you can draw benefits from your pension between the ages of 55 and 75. There are some minor exceptions to this, but most people will be in this age range when they retire. This legal position doesn't mean your pension scheme automatically *has* to allow you to retire between these ages. If you have a company pension, the commencement date may be linked to when you would be expected to retire from that job.

However, nearly all forms of personal pension and an increasing number of company pensions have a flexible retirement age that allows you to choose when you take benefits between the legal upper and lower limits.

The fact that you may be able to draw pension benefits and carry on working, or carry on working and delay taking benefits, gives you a great deal of flexibility when it comes to planning your retirement finances. You could continue to work part time and draw all or part of your pension. Alternatively you may prefer to continue working full time and delay taking your pension benefits, thereby avoiding paying Income Tax on income you don't need.

You can even delay taking your state pension. Why would you want to do this? The answer is that for every five weeks you delay taking it, the state pension increases by 1%, which equates to an annual increase of 10.4%.

If you bear in mind that this increase is guaranteed and will increase with inflation for the rest of your life, it may be worth considering.

_____

Three stages

This book is about managing your finances in retirement. It is not about planning a lifestyle, but giving some consideration to this will help you with your pension plans.

....

Insight

Inevitably things will change as your life moves on, sometimes more quickly then you expect. I have had clients who were
(Contd)

adamant that they would never work again, only to be back in the same job within months, not because they had to, but because they wanted to.

As already touched upon, the old clear distinction between working and retirement has become somewhat blurred and it may help to think about your retirement in three overlapping stages.

▶ **Stage one, the early years:** *At this stage of retirement we are still fit and healthy and often undertake some form of physical activity, such as part-time or voluntary work, or actively pursue a hobby or long-held ambition.*
▶ **Stage two, the middle years:** *This stage most closely aligns to our traditional view of retirement, whereby most of us will still be reasonably fit and healthy but perhaps not as active as we once were, although we will still want to pursue hobbies and interests.*
▶ **Stage three, the later years:** *At this stage, we will have slowed down considerably and may even need support from others.*

Insight

Each of these three stages may need a different level of income, and in practice the stages will overlap. For most of us it will be impossible to be precise about our requirements for each, but thinking in this way helps us to give some consideration to how much income we may need at various stages of our retirement.

Finances in stage one

If you are continuing to work, on either a full- or part-time basis, you may not need to take benefits from all or some of your pensions in order to generate the income you need.

On the other hand, if you are stopping work, you will almost certainly need to draw on your pension(s) and may need capital to fulfil that lifetime ambition. You need to give some thought to whether you will need more or less income than in stages two and three.

Finances in stage two

At this stage, it is assumed that if you have been working, you have decided to stop work altogether, and whilst you are still fit and active you are beginning to slow down a little.

If you haven't drawn your pension yet, you will almost certainly need to do so now. Depending on what you intend to do with your leisure time, you may find that you need less money than in stage one.

On the income side of things, if you have been drawing a pension for some time, you may find that unless your pension has some level of inflation protection, the real value of your income will have started to fall.

Finances in stage three

Stage three assumes you are now not so active as you were in previous stages, so on one level you may not need so much income. Against that you may need to pay for help of some description.

Unless you have a pension with full inflation protection, your buying power will almost certainly have been reduced and you may need to start eating into your capital. You may also have to raise additional capital in some way, such as moving to a smaller home or raising capital through equity release.

Insight

Equity release is the term used for using part of the value of your home to improve your income. It is a very emotive subject for a number of reasons, including the fear of not leaving an inheritance, the fear of building up a debt higher than the value of your home, and last but not least the less than glorious reputation surrounding this way of raising money.

Chapter 14 explains how this is no longer the case, especially in the later years of retirement, but the key point when you first retire is not to dismiss the possibility of equity release out of hand as even if it is not right for you now, using it to generate funds later can impact on other decisions you make now.

Should you stay or should you go?

Insight

As already mentioned, the old distinctions between work and retirement have become blurred. Nowhere is this more evident than in the area of work. An increasing number of my clients are choosing to work beyond their 'retirement date'. In the main this is because they want to work rather than because they have to. Even some of those who couldn't wait to retire are back working after a few months and sometimes in the same job that they couldn't wait to leave! The next section gives some advice on this area.

One of the biggest choices you may face when approaching retirement is whether or not you will continue to work in some form or another, and it may be worth asking yourself the following questions:

- ▶ *Do I want to or do I have to leave my current job?*
- ▶ *Will I continue in my current job but work part time?*
- ▶ *Will I continue to work but do something different?*
- ▶ *Can I afford to stop working?*
- ▶ *Will I be able to continue working?*
- ▶ *What will I do with my time?*
- ▶ *Will I be able to work?*

Each of these points is explained in a little more detail below.

Do I want to or do I have to leave my current job?

You may have been counting down the days until you can leave your current job. Alternatively you may dread the day when something you love doing will stop. In all probability you will fall somewhere in between.

You might not have any alternative but to leave work, although more and more employers no longer have a compulsory retirement age.

Legislation is also continually changing, meaning that the idea of a fixed retirement age is gradually becoming a thing of the past. Naturally, if you are self-employed or own your business then the choice will usually be yours.

If you want to keep working and you can, then the issue is fairly clear cut: keep on doing so. On the other hand, if you can't wait to leave then your decision is also fairly clear, but bear in mind some people who couldn't wait to leave a job find that after a short period of time they wish they hadn't.

If you are not sure, the decision is not so easy. If you continue working then you can always change your mind, but if you leave and want to go back you may find the door firmly shut.

Insight

This raises one of the most, if not the single most important thing about retirement planning, in that many of the decisions you make at this time will have an impact on you for the rest of your life. Furthermore, once many of these decisions have been made they can be difficult if not impossible to change or reverse.

The advice is that if you are not sure you want to continue working, set yourself a time limit to continue working to see how you feel. You may find that because you don't *have* to work then you have a totally different perspective on it.

Will I continue in my current job but work part time?

You may want and be able to work part time in the same role as you do now, or take on less stressful work connected with your current role. For example, the person who prepares my tax returns started his business when he retired from his job as a tax inspector.

Needless to say, if you go down this route your income will probably be reduced, but as already mentioned there is nothing to prevent you working and drawing your pension at the same time.

Will I continue to work but do something different?

Retiring from a particular job doesn't necessarily mean stopping work altogether, in fact it can open up a whole new world of opportunity to do something completely different. It can provide the chance to earn an income pursuing a hobby that you enjoy but couldn't previously earn a living from simply because it wouldn't generate sufficient income.

You may have had a lifetime interest in a hobby that has made you extremely knowledgeable about that subject and that knowledge may well have a value. A friend's father who used to be a bank manager supplemented his pension income by buying and selling railway memorabilia.

Alternatively you may have a skill that will also enable you to earn a living or supplement your income. That skill may be specialist or mundane. I have a client who is an extremely skilled woodworker who supplements his income by producing intricate carvings. Another client who used to be an office manager does decorating from time to time, and a former headmaster I know drives a van for a brewery!

You will need to pay tax on this income, but if you are self-employed you will also be able to offset certain expenses against it. How this works is beyond the scope of this book but other books in this series including *Set Up a Small Business* and *Understand Tax for Small Businesses* (Teach Yourself) cover the subject very well.

Can I afford to stop working?

You may be faced with the situation where your retirement income is insufficient to meet your ongoing commitments. Your mortgage may have a few more years to run or you may have an interest-only mortgage that has an amount outstanding to pay. Once again at this stage the objective is not to quantify in detail the amounts involved but rather to give some thought as to whether this will be an issue.

Will I be able to continue working?

Up until this point the assumption has been that you will be in the fortunate position of being able to choose whether or not you will be able to work. It may well be that you do not have this choice, you may suffer from poor health or simply be unable to secure work.

On the face of it, it may seem that you have no choice other than to retire and draw your pension(s), but once again this assumes that retiring and drawing your pension *have* to be linked which is not the case.

You may be entitled to state benefits that could mean delaying taking some or all of your pension(s), resulting in an increase in your pension benefits. Whilst this may not be practical it is always worth investigating.

What will you do with your leisure time?

Insight

What you do with your leisure time will have a major impact on how much money you will need and on the way you take the benefits from your pension, savings or investments. Personally I have a long-held desire to build a model railway in my garden and also spend time touring around Europe. Modest ambitions maybe, but there will be an initial and ongoing cost. At the same time, circumstances permitting, I intend to work part time as long as I can and still enjoy doing so, meaning I can use at least some of the money I currently spend on mortgage payments to fund our increased leisure costs.

Retirement can be a time where you have the opportunity to fulfil a lifetime ambition, spend a bit more time on a hobby or just relax. What, where, how and for how long you intend to do so will have a major impact on how much income you will need.

The cost of buying a Winnebago and spending five years exploring the USA is likely to be substantially more expensive than midweek walking holidays in the Highlands.

If you have a hobby that you intend to pursue this could result in significant expenditure – even watching the TV can result in higher heating bills.

Giving some thought to what you want to do will enable you to estimate what it will cost. In turn this will help you decide in what form to take your retirement benefits.

What will retirement mean to you?

The tables below are designed to help you marshal your thoughts on the points above and formulate what retirement means to you personally. At this point don't worry about trying to quantify the cost of this or even being definitive about what you will do at any given point in retirement. The objective of the exercise is to enable you to start giving some thought to what your personal retirement will be like. When you read the chapters that follow you will be able to relate the content to your own situation.

Work

Will you carry on working?	Yes	No	Not sure
Full time in the same job Part time in the same job Full time in another job Part time in another job Will not work at all			
If you carry on working, at what age do you intend to stop?			
If you carry on working, do you intend to wind down over time? If so, what are your plans?			

Home and leisure
If you have given any thought to how you will spend your leisure time, use the activity column in the table below to write down what the activity will be. If you can quantify the capital or ongoing

costs, put an estimate in each of the two costs columns. If at this stage you are not sure of the cost, just put a yes, no or not sure.

Use the final column to note how this may change over the years. The first two rows are examples.

Activity	Will it involve a capital cost?	Will it involve an ongoing cost?	How will this change over the years?
Build model railway	Yes, but not sure how much	Very little	Probably not
Go around Europe	Buy caravan £10–£15,000	Say £5,000 a year	Not sure how long will do this for

TEN POINTS TO REMEMBER

1 *The traditional view of retirement is in many ways out of date and may not apply to you.*

2 *For many people retirement can be broken down into three key stages:*
   ▷ *The early years – when you will hopefully be fit and healthy, may want to work in some shape or form and actively pursue leisure activities.*
   ▷ *The middle years – the stage most akin to the traditional view of retirement when you will be slowing down but still reasonably active.*
   ▷ *The later years – you will not be so active and may need support from others.*

3 *The legal position is that you can draw your pension between the ages of 55 and 75 although some company pension schemes still have a stated retirement age.*

4 *You can work and draw your pension.*

5 *If you are continuing to work it may be possible to delay taking your pension.*

6 *You should give some thought as to whether you want to work, either in your current job or do something completely different.*

7 *Consider whether you have a hobby or skill that you could use to produce an income.*

8 *Thinking how you will spend your leisure time will help you decide how to take your pension benefit and plan your expenditure.*

9 *If you are unsure whether or not to continue working it may be easier to carry on until you make your mind up rather than go back later.*

10 *Many of the decisions you make about your retirement will stay with you for the rest of your life. As these can be difficult or sometimes impossible to reverse it is important not to rush into any decision.*

2

Things to consider and research

In this chapter you will learn about:
- *the different ways in which you can take benefits from a pension*
- *spouse's pensions*
- *using capital in your home*
- *gathering information and tracking down pensions and savings plans*

Insight

One of the problems when you retire is the sheer number of choices you have to make, particularly in the way you can take benefits from some types of pension. One way of making this a little easier is first to give some thought to how you would want to take benefits in a perfect world and then work out where you would be prepared to compromise.

Some company pension schemes will only allow you to take benefits in a certain format, for example they may dictate the amount of pension that will be paid to your husband or wife if you die before them, and the amount the pension will increase each year (if at all).

Most personal pensions and many company pensions are far more flexible offering a wide range of choice. Whatever type of pension you have, you will have a number of decisions to make.

Later chapters will explain in detail the choices you have when it comes to taking benefits from a pension, but before we look at the technicalities the first part of this chapter will explain what you may need to think about to make sense of the choices you may face. These may include whether you should:

- ▶ *delay or take your pension benefits*
- ▶ *take a lump sum or increased pension*
- ▶ *take a level or increasing pension*
- ▶ *take a pension that is guaranteed for life or could rise or fall*
- ▶ *take a spouse's pension*
- ▶ *risk eroding your capital to increase your income*
- ▶ *consider releasing capital from your home.*

The second part of this chapter will then go on to suggest what information you may need to gather in order to start making those choices.

Should you delay taking benefits from your pension?

Insight

The usual assumption is that you have to take benefits from a pension at a certain age, but more often than not this is no longer the case and you will have a degree of flexibility about when you take benefits. If you have this choice and you don't need the income, for example if you are continuing to work, then you will need to weigh up the benefits of taking the pension at the original date or delaying in order to receive a greater income later.

If you don't need the income from a pension then you will need to decide what to do about any pension that is due to start on your original retirement date. Different pensions have different rules but most will fall into one of the following categories.

- ▶ *pensions that you have to take at a certain age*
- ▶ *pensions that you can delay taking and will definitely increase in value*
- ▶ *pensions that you can delay taking and may increase or fall in value.*

If you have a pension that you must take at a certain age then on the surface of things you are faced with little choice. However, it may be possible to move it to one that will allow you to vary the date you take benefits. Whether this is a good idea or not is a different question and in most cases will require specialist advice.

It is always worth finding out if you *must* take your pension on a certain date and if you delay taking benefits will they increase and if so by how much? Rules change over a period of time and you may have more choice than you originally thought.

If you don't need the income, you have a pension that will definitely increase in value and you can delay taking benefits, it is worth considering doing so. The reason for this is, apart from having a higher pension when you do take benefits, taking pension income will be added to your other income and you may pay tax on income you don't need.

Against that you will have to work out the impact of losing the income for the years that you haven't taken the benefits, income you could use to save or spend as you wish.

This ability to delay taking your pension is more common than you may think. Most public sector schemes have this facility, as does the state pension scheme.

If you have a pension that you can delay taking benefits from, but that pension could fall in value, then you need to investigate if you can alter it so this is unlikely to happen.

___

Should you take a lump sum from pensions?

Most pensions will allow you to take a tax-free lump sum on retirement, but you should be aware that doing so nearly always means giving up some pension income.

From a purely financial point of view, whether or not this is good value will largely depend on the type of pension you have.

Irrespective of whether taking a lump sum or a higher income provides the greatest value, you may have no alternative but to take a lump sum, for instance you may need it to pay off your mortgage.

Finally, emotions are at least as important as hard facts in decisions such as these and you may want to take a lump sum even if from a purely financial sense you would be better off taking an increased income. For this reason the vast majority of people take the lump sum.

Until you have the hard facts and figures it is unlikely you will be able to decide. To help formulate an answer it's worth considering the following:

- *Have you no alternative but to take the lump sum?*
- *Would you take the lump sum instead of an increased income:*
  - *if it made more financial sense not to?*
  - *if it was better value to take it?*
  - *if there was no difference in value?*
- *Would you take the lump sum irrespective of value?*

Should you take a level or an increasing pension?

Some pensions will give you the choice of taking a higher income that will not increase or a lower income at outset that will increase over the years. The problem with the former is that over the years the income will be eroded by inflation.

In practice, you will need to see the figures to make a final decision, but if you had to make a choice would you prefer:

- *an income that starts higher but over the years will be eroded by inflation?*
- *an income that starts lower but will increase?*

Insight

Whilst the figures vary, assuming increases of 3% a year,
it often takes 12–13 years for an increasing pension to catch
up with a level one and about 20 years for the total amount
you receive to be equal. Therefore you need to live for 20 years
before you would be better off taking an increasing pension.
Even if this is the case, if you think you will need more income
in stage one of retirement then you may still prefer the higher
income to start with.

Do you want a pension where you can vary the income?

As explained when we were looking at the three stages of
retirement, you may not have the same income needs throughout
retirement. You may prefer to have more income in the earlier
stages of retirement when you are more likely to be fit and healthy
or want to do something special, or you may prefer a higher
income later in life to be able to afford the best quality care if you
are unable to look after yourself fully.

If you are uncertain as to what income you may require at
different stages of retirement you may want to be able to vary
your income.

Bearing this in mind do you think you would prefer:

▶ *a higher income in the earlier years of retirement?*
▶ *a higher income in the later years?*
▶ *a level income throughout?*
▶ *the ability to vary income?*

Or perhaps you are not yet sure and need to look more closely at
the numbers?

Will you need a spouse's pension?

Some pensions will automatically pay a pension to your husband or wife if you die before them. Others will give you a choice of whether or not you can take a spouse's pension and the amount.

> ### Insight
> Whether you need a spouse's pension will largely depend on your partner's own retirement finances. If they have sufficient income in their own right, then they will not need to rely on your pension if you die before them. In this case, if you have a choice it may be worth considering a higher pension that will stop on your death.

On the other hand, they may be entirely dependent on your pension, in which case you will need a pension that will continue to pay an income for both of your lives.

Where you have this choice, taking a spouse's pension will usually mean a reduction in your own pension, but the exact amounts will depend on your own and your partner's age and state of health.

If you have the type of pension that will automatically pay a spouse's pension, then even if you don't want or need a spouse's pension it is highly unlikely the amount of pension paid to you will be increased. Whilst it may be possible to transfer to a pension where you do not have to take a spouse's pension it will rarely pay you to do so.

Based on this, if you have a choice consider the following:

▶ *Will you need a pension that will continue to be paid to your husband or wife if you die before them?*
▶ *How much pension will your spouse or partner require if you die before them?*

Are you willing to risk your capital in order to obtain an increased income?

One of the big fears many people have when they retire is that they will run out of money before they die.

Insight

One of the features of all pensions is that the pension has to be paid as long as you live, but some types of pension allow you the potential to take a bigger income initially but at the risk of that income being reduced in the future.

Whilst it may be foolish to spend all of your capital in the early years of retirement, you may wish to consider the following:

▶ *Whilst pensions have to guarantee an income for the rest of your life you may want to consider a pension that is linked to an investment. The advantage of this type of pension is that initially you will usually be able to secure a higher income than a guaranteed pension but there is a risk that your capital could be eroded and you could end up with a lower pension.*

▶ *You may want to use some of your savings to boost your income. Even if you only take the interest, over time the value of your income will be eroded by inflation. If you take more than the interest then your capital will also reduce but you may be prepared to do this in order to improve your standard of living in the early years of retirement.*

Insight

Eroding your capital can be worth considering, especially if you only have to do it for a short while. You may retire before state retirement age in which case your state pension will commence at a later date and increase your income, or you may anticipate receiving a lump sum, perhaps from an inheritance, although bear in mind you cannot always guarantee you will actually receive what you have anticipated.

► *In order to increase your income or grow your capital you may want to consider some form of investment that offers the potential for a greater return than a deposit account but with some risk to your capital.*

Insight

At the time of writing it is very difficult to obtain anything other than a miserly rate of interest on deposit savings. Even when interest rates are 'normal', obtaining an attractive real rate over and above inflation can be difficult. This may mean that you will want or need to seek a higher return on your money. Despite what the advert or the person encouraging you to take out a product says, there is nearly always a catch. It could mean tying your money up for a period of time, or losing interest whenever you make a withdrawal, or it may involve some risk to your capital. There is nothing inherently wrong with this as long as you know what the catches are. The advice therefore is to always make sure that any disadvantages are clearly highlighted to you in writing.

► *Although I very much hope that you are in good health as you read this, the fact has to be faced that not everyone will be, and as we get older we will tend to suffer from some form of illness or other. This could mean that either now or at some stage in the future you will be prepared to trade some or all of your capital to increase the quality of your life.*

► *The state benefit system provides a safety net of minimum income. At present a married couple, where one is over the age of 65, can expect a minimum income of £198.45 a week. This can be increased up to £266 a week if you have some savings. As you might expect the rules surrounding this are rather complex, and not everyone is eligible, but if you are close to being entitled to these state benefits you may wish to consider eroding or risk eroding your capital in the knowledge that there is a safety net in place.*

   ▷ *What are your views on eroding or risking your capital?*
   ▷ *Would you be prepared to take some risk to increase your standard of living in the knowledge that this*

could mean reducing your income or capital if the investment fell in value?

Insight

I worked out a long time ago that whilst I may be able to retire at 65 and have a reasonable standard of living through 'traditional' pension planning, I simply couldn't save enough money to have the standard of living I would want. One of the ways of dealing with this will be to take my pension and invest in such a way that I will be able to increase my income. Doing this will mean there is a high risk that my capital will be eroded. I accept this in the knowledge that if I live to the point where this becomes an issue I will be able to raise additional capital through my house either by trading down or by equity release.

Are you willing or able to use the capital in your home?

If you own your own home then it may be possible for you to use the value built up in order to release capital or increase your income.

One example of this would be trading down to a less expensive home in which case you may well have additional capital which you can use to boost your standard of living. However, in my experience, far more people if they do trade down at all, do so some years into retirement, and the main reason for doing so is not to raise money but to move to a smaller more manageable home.

Even if you have no immediate plans to move it is worth considering if you may be willing to release capital from your home at some stage in the future. There are two main ways of doing this, either by trading down or by equity release.

Insight

Equity release is the term used to raise capital from your home whilst continuing to live there. Whilst there are exceptions to the general rule, my opinion is that in most cases you need to be aged 70–75 before the economics of doing this start to stack up. As with all generalizations there will be exceptions and there can be circumstances where it is worth considering at ages as young as 50, although I would consider these to be rare.

The reason for considering this point when you first retire is not so much to decide if you will take this option immediately, but rather if you are prepared to consider it later then it can help you make the other choices you have to make now.

For example, you may feel more comfortable taking a higher pension that will not increase with inflation as opposed to a lower pension that will.

In a similar way you may be prepared to erode your capital or take on some investment risk in order to increase your immediate income in the knowledge that, if needs be, you can replace some or all of that capital with money raised on your home.

Insight

In my experience people discount equity release for two main reasons. Firstly, it has a terrible reputation for being a 'con' and secondly many feel that by doing so they are depriving their children of their inheritance. With regard to the former, most modern equity release products bear no resemblance to their earlier forebears and whilst they may not always be right for a particular individual, the product itself is an honest one.

With regard to the latter point, more often than not in my experience, the children who will benefit from any inheritance are more concerned about their parents' standard of living than any money they may or may not receive when their parents are dead.

▶ *Will you be taking capital from your home when you first retire?*
▶ *Would you consider taking capital from your home at a later stage of retirement?*

Gathering information

In order to consider your retirement options fully you will need to obtain information on your pensions and your other finances. Subsequent chapters will explain in more detail how to use that information, but for the present we will consider what information is needed and why it is needed.

As well as explaining what information you need to gather, this section will also explain how to track down missing information.

You will need to obtain details of:

▶ *your pensions including*
  ▷ *state pension*
  ▷ *current and previous company pensions*
  ▷ *current and previous personal pensions*
▶ *any outstanding mortgages*
▶ *savings accounts and plans*
▶ *investments.*

Insight

Some pensions, such as final salary schemes, give very little choice about how to take benefits, so obtaining and using the information you need is relatively easy. However, other types of company and personal pensions have a wide range of choices, none of which on their own are particularly confusing, but when these are put together an overwhelming number of choices is created. If you consult an adviser they will ask you a series of questions similar to those asked

(Contd)

earlier in this chapter and this will narrow down these
choices to help you make a decision.

STATE PENSION

How to obtain the information
If you are approaching the state retirement age you will
automatically be sent details of how much state pension you will
receive and asked if you want to take the pension or delay it.

If you have not received this you can complete a form BR19 and send
this to The Pension Service for a forecast. You can obtain this form
online or by phone (the contact details are at the end of this book).

Why do you need this information?
Although often derided, the state pension can form a significant
part of your income in retirement and is guaranteed. Knowing
what this income will be can help make decisions in other areas
including what risks you may want to take with other pensions.

Even if you are some time away from state retirement age, knowing
how much income will commence at that time will help you decide
how to make up any shortfall in the interim.

Insight
If you retire a few years before state retirement age, then
knowing how much state pension you will be entitled to
can make planning in the interim a lot easier. A couple's
joint state pension income will often exceed £10,000 a year.
Knowing you have this amount of income starting in a few
years might mean that you will be prepared to use some of
your capital in the interim.

CURRENT AND PREVIOUS COMPANY PENSIONS

If you are approaching the retirement age for a company pension
scheme, you should automatically be sent details of what pension

you will receive. If you don't receive this you will need to request it from your pension provider.

> **Note:** I will frequently use the expression 'provider' throughout this book. What I mean by this is the organization that provides your pension or investment. This single term could apply to your employer, an insurance company or investment company.

What information do you need?

The information you will need depends on the type of pension you have. If you have a final salary scheme (either as a current or former member) you will need to know:

▶ *what pension you will receive*
▶ *what lump sum you are entitled to and how much pension you have to give up to get it*
▶ *whether the pension will increase*
▶ *the amount of any spouse's pension.*

If you don't need the benefits from this or these pensions then it is also worth finding out whether, if you delay taking benefits, they will increase and if so by how much.

Insight

Many pensions allow you to delay taking benefits. In doing so you need to weigh up the benefits of any increase in pension against losing out on income starting straight away. This needs to be calculated individually but can be worthwhile. Recently a client of mine who was still working beyond retirement age delayed taking her previous company and state pensions for just one year. As a result her state pension increased by 10.4% and her company pension by 8.5%.

With a final salary pension you will not usually have any choice over how the benefits are paid other than whether or not to take a lump sum.

However, if you have a personal pension or a company pension that is not an average or final salary one (this will be explained more fully in Chapter 4), you almost certainly have a number of choices including:

▶ *whether to take the pension with the existing company or shop around for a better rate*
▶ *whether or not to take a spouse's pension*
▶ *whether or not to take a level or increasing pension.*

PERSONAL PENSIONS

Most personal pension providers will have a standard pack that they will send out either on request or close to the date that you originally stated that you intended to take benefits.

These packs will typically contain information on:

▶ *the value of the pension fund*
▶ *the amount of pension your existing pension provider will pay*
▶ *if there is any penalty if you move your pension to another provider*
▶ *how much lump sum is available*
▶ *what pension choices you have, e.g. a pension that will increase or stay level, pay a spouse's or single pension.*

These packs may not always contain all the information you need. They may not show the pension in the format you want to take it, but asking for one of these packs is a good place to start. If you then require some different information you can specifically ask for it.

Insight

You don't have to take your pension with your existing provider. You can often obtain a higher pension by shopping around.

SAVINGS AND INVESTMENTS

Retirement is an ideal time to review your existing savings and investments as you may want to start using these to support your lifestyle and some changes may be required.

Initially you will just need to know the value of the investment, but it is also worth considering:

▶ *Is the investment still appropriate in terms of investment risk?*
▶ *Is it possible to take an income from it?*
▶ *Is it possible to alter it in any way without having to cancel it?*
▶ *How is the investment taxed?*

These points will be explained in later chapters.

You should also obtain up-to-date projections of savings plans such as endowments that are due to pay out at some stage in the future.

MORTGAGES AND OTHER LOANS

If your mortgage is still outstanding you need to check:

▶ *the exact date it is due to be paid*
▶ *the outstanding balance*
▶ *the monthly repayments.*

The reason for this is that you may want to pay your mortgage off, and if not you will need to take into account how much it will cost to pay it until it is due to be repaid.

If you have an interest only mortgage you will need to work out how it will be repaid. You may have an endowment that will pay some of it but still have a shortfall. Alternatively you may not have anything in place to pay it off. In both cases you will need to consider if you will use any lump sums from your pension or other source, or continue to make the interest payments indefinitely.

The same principle applies to any other loans, including credit cards.

Tracking down pensions and savings plans

It has been estimated that there are £15 billion of unclaimed assets in the UK, with £452 million in National Savings alone. This is money that people have lost track of for a number of reasons: they may have moved or simply forgotten that they had the savings in the first place.

The good news is that it is often relatively easy to track down this money and there are a number of organizations that can help.

For National Savings (including Premium Bonds), bank and building society accounts there is a single website: www.mylostaccount.co.uk. If you would rather make enquiries by phone or post there are separate address and contact numbers for National Savings, bank and building society accounts (details are given in the further help section at the end of the book).

For pensions there is a tracing service run by the Department of Work and Pensions (again details are given at the end of the book).

Many other forms of savings and investments can be traced using the Unclaimed Assets Register (UAR) which holds information on many life policies, pensions, Unit Trust holdings and share dividends. The UAR makes a small charge for their service which at the time of writing is £25. (The details of these sources of information are given in the further help section at the end of this book.)

Conclusion

You will have many choices to make when you retire and this chapter has been about helping you to start considering what you will do with these choices. In practice, you will not be able to give definitive answers until you know the amounts involved, but giving some thought in advance will help you make a start.

TEN POINTS TO REMEMBER

1 When you retire you will have a number of choices to make about how you take your pension benefits.

2 The amount of choice will depend on the type of pension scheme, but could include whether to take:
   ▷ a lump sum or increased pension
   ▷ a level or increasing pension
   ▷ a pension that is guaranteed for life or could rise or fall
   ▷ a pension that will continue to be paid to your spouse if you die before them.

3 You don't have to take your pension when you retire.

4 You can also take your pension and keep working.

5 If you decide to delay taking your pension you will need to find out if it will definitely increase in value or whether it could fall.

6 You don't have to take your pension with your existing provider. If you have a final salary pension it is unlikely you will be able to obtain a better deal elsewhere but if you have a personal pension there is a high probability you will.

7 You will need to gather details of your:
   ▷ state pension
   ▷ company pensions
   ▷ personal pensions
   ▷ savings and investments
   ▷ mortgages and other loans.

8 You need to give some thought as to whether you would be prepared to eat into your capital to improve your standard of living.

9 *Think about whether later in retirement you would be prepared to move home or use equity release to improve your standard of living.*

10 *There are £15 billion in unclaimed assets in the UK – some of that money might be yours.*

3

....

How much money will you need?

In this chapter you will:
- *examine your current expenditure*
- *estimate your retirement income requirements*

Given that most people have never retired before, it is not surprising that they have little idea of what income they will need in retirement. On first thought the question may seem irrelevant as most people will adjust their spending to match their income.

However, you may have a number of choices over how much income you receive. For example, you may obtain a higher return on your savings by investing them in stocks and shares rather than in a deposit account.

Also, whilst some pensions give little choice over how you can take benefits, others give a great deal of choice as shown in the example below.

Example
Ian Wainwright has built up a personal pension fund of £100,000. He has a number of choices over how he can turn that into a pension. If he doesn't take a lump sum, takes a pension that will stop when he dies and doesn't increase at all, it will pay him £6,915 a year. On the other hand if he takes the maximum lump sum, a pension that will pay the same amount to his wife if he dies before her and the pension increases by 3% a year, he will only receive £2,731.

Estimating your expenditure

Once you have given some thought to what retirement means to you, you can then turn your attention to how much money you will need in order to make that desired way of life a reality.

The probability is that in retirement your income will be lower than when you were working. If one of your main worries about retirement is what standard of living you can expect, then you are not alone.

Changes in how you will be taxed may affect how much income you need. You may find you pay less tax and National Insurance when you are retired, but the starting point is to work out what your expenditure will be.

Insight

Every textbook that has ever been written on personal finance stresses the importance of budgeting, but in practice few of us do it. This is because we live in the real world rather than a textbook and most of us know what our income is and live within it. However, retirement is a time when it really does pay to invest some time into this exercise as it:

▶ *may reassure you about the level of income you actually need*
▶ *will highlight those areas of expenditure you can adjust if you have to economize.*

Some people find working out the amount they spend relatively easy. Far more of us have varying degrees of difficulty, ranging from 'it is a bit of an effort but it can be done' through to finding it virtually impossible. If you fall into this latter category you are not alone and the method suggested in this chapter should help.

Insight

I find the easiest way of helping people work out what their expenditure in retirement will be is to take their current expenditure and just make adjustments for the large items that are likely to change. In most instances this is restricted to:

- *mortgage payments*
- *the costs of motoring*
- *the cost of commuting*

To go into any more detail than this would be incredibly difficult and would serve little purpose. The challenge is not so much working out what your expenditure will be in retirement, but working out what it is now.

HOW TO WORK OUT YOUR CURRENT EXPENDITURE

When we are asked to break down our expenditure most of us, including me, first hesitate and then make a guess.

At the end of this chapter is a table that you can use to enter details of your expenditure. Working out how much to put in each box can be extremely difficult, but there is a way to make the task a little easier.

Before thinking about *what* you spend your money on, first give some thought to *how* you pay for things. Do you use cash, debit cards, credit cards or all of these and more? How do you settle your bills – by direct debit or do you send a cheque?

The reason for doing this is that unless you pay for most things by cash, working out *how* you spend your money will identify where the records are that will show you *what* you spend your money on.

In most cases, three months' bank statements and credits card will provide most if not all of the information you need. When you have those statements you can start entering the amounts in the expenditure checklist at the end of this chapter.

For example, if you pay for your shopping by cheque or debit card this will appear on your statement as Sainsbury's, Tesco's etc.

If you look at the expenditure chart you will see a row headed 'supermarket'. There is no need to be too precise about whether you spend the money on food, drink, washing-up liquid or even loo rolls, the point is that you spend that money each week or month, so just enter the figure in the 'supermarket' box.

What is a little harder to identify is where the money that is not itemized in this way goes, and there are two ways to go about this. The first is to keep a log of how much you spend on items such as parking, going to the pub on a Friday, or even the odd coffee. The problem with this approach is that if you are the type of person that is comfortable doing this, then you probably already know how much you spend and what you spend it on.

If you can clearly identify where this money goes then enter it in the appropriate box. If not, one simple way of dealing with this is to enter all cash withdrawals in the 'cash/other' box. In some respects it doesn't matter what you spend the money on, the fact is that you spend it on something!

The second chart is for single expenditure on items such as holidays, Christmas, buying a new car or even home maintenance.

WORKING OUT WHAT YOU WILL SPEND IN RETIREMENT

When you have worked out how much you spend now, you can then estimate how this will be different in retirement. Once again this isn't an easy exercise, apart from anything else, never having been retired before means that you will not know how much you will spend.

Some changes in expenditure will precisely coincide with your retirement, others will not. For example, your commuting costs may stop completely whereas your mortgage may continue for some time or may have been paid off several years ago.

The table below gives some ideas of those items that may or may not change once you have retired.

Travel expenses	Unless you are continuing to work, commuting costs will tend to reduce but you may spend more on leisure mileage. You may also be able to obtain subsidized transport, such as the famous bus pass. If you run two cars now, you may only need one when you retire.
Mortgage	If your mortgage coincides with your retirement, then this will be an obvious item that will reduce. If you have already finished paying your mortgage this will not be a factor. If your mortgage runs into retirement you need to calculate if it would be best to pay it off as a lump sum or continue paying it.
Other loans	As well as a mortgage you may have other debts that you want to repay or you may even need to borrow some money, for example to buy a new car. Points that may apply to you could include: ▶ *Do you need to pay off a credit card or cards?* ▶ *Do you need to borrow money for some other purpose?* ▶ *Do you still have ongoing costs for children or grandchildren such as university costs?*
Heat and light	If you are going to spend more time at home the probability is that these costs will increase rather than reduce. It is unlikely you will be able to quantify this until you actually start having to settle the bills. As a starting point it is suggested you budget for the same amount as you spend now.

(Contd)

Food and drink	Unless there is a specific reason for a major change, such as not needing to pay for lunch, then use the same costs as now.
Leisure	If you intend to stop working or work part time you will have more time for leisure. There is likely to be a cost to this so you need to consider: ▶ *Is there anything you are likely to do that will result in a capital outlay?* ▶ *Is there anything that will have an ongoing cost? Is this likely to change over the years?*
Holidays	This will totally depend on you. Some people will spend more, others will spend less. Refer back to the earlier section on what you intend to do in retirement.
Life assurance, health cover and pensions	If you are going to take benefits from your pension then you will no longer be paying into it, so this should be deducted. Life and health assurance may finish at this time, so once again the cost of these will need to be deducted.
One-off expenditure	On retirement you may have one or more items of capital expenditure that are unlikely to be repeated. Examples could include buying a holiday home or a holiday of a lifetime.

PUTTING IN THE NUMBERS

Use the chart below to itemize your regular expenditure both now and when retired.

Insight

When you have completed this task you may find the amount is far higher than you expected or far lower. If this is the case, don't worry. Both of these outcomes are very common. If the expenditure is higher than your income, completing the table will help identify areas where you may need to economize. If it is lower this is probably due to small daily expenditure that we all make, but find it hard to keep track of. In this case, enter the difference between your income and expenditure in the 'cash/other' box.

Expenditure item	Now	Retired

Mortgage/rent
Utilities (either enter as a single item or
  break down)
  ▶ *gas*
  ▶ *electric*
  ▶ *home phone and broadband*
  ▶ *mobile phone*		

Council tax		
Supermarket shop		
Credit card payments		
Loan repayments		
Life insurance		
Home insurance		
Pensions		

Motoring (either enter as a single item
  or break down)
  ▶ *car tax*
  ▶ *car servicing*
  ▶ *car insurance*
  ▶ *petrol*		

(Contd)

Expenditure item	Now	Retired
Travel (not covered under motoring)		
Petrol		
Clothes		
Home and garden maintenance		
Leisure and entertainment (but not holidays)		
Cash/other		

As well as regular expenditure, most of us have irregular costs that may be a one-off or occur say once a year. Use the chart below to enter these items.

In the first column list some of these items, in the second enter an amount (you may have to estimate this amount) and in the third write how often this will occur. For example, paying off your mortgage will be a one-off, but Christmas is an annual event.

Insight

Take care that you don't double count items that may also be entered in the regular expenditure table above. The most common example of this is if you take out a loan or put items such as Christmas expenditure on your credit card.

The bottom rows have been left blank for you to enter other items that apply to you.

Item	Cost	Frequency
Pay off mortgage		
Pay off other loans		
Move house		
Buy new car		
Holiday home		
Home improvements		

Item	Cost	Frequency
Fund hobby or ambition		
Christmas		
Birthdays		

TEN POINTS TO REMEMBER

1 *Although your income will dictate how much you can spend, it is still worth estimating your likely expenditure.*

2 *By doing this you will be able to identify those areas where you may be able to economize.*

3 *You may find you pay less tax and National Insurance when you are retired.*

4 *The starting point is to work out your current expenditure.*

5 *By identifying in what way you spend your money you will be able to ascertain what you spend it on.*

6 *In the main, costs that are likely to reduce are:*
   ▷ *mortgage*
   ▷ *motoring*
   ▷ *commuting*

7 *The main costs that could increase are:*
   ▷ *heat and light*
   ▷ *leisure and entertainment*

8 *You may incur one-off costs such as buying a holiday home or having to buy a new car.*

9 *Take care to include irregular costs such as holidays and Christmas.*

10 *Don't worry if you can't identify all of your spending, just enter it in the 'other' box.*

4

Understanding pensions

In this chapter you will learn about:
- *what types of pension exist*
- *some specific pension types*
- *contributions to pensions*
- *the state pension*
- *pension credits*

Insight

As well as advising clients on retirement planning, I also teach other financial advisers about pensions. To be honest, some of the issues are so complex that even those who have worked in the business for many years struggle to understand the detail. The good news is that for you to understand what is needed to effectively plan for retirement, you don't need to go into a great deal of detail and for all of the variations on a theme there are only three types of pension.

A pension is only one of the many ways that a person can save for retirement. On the plus side, they will sometimes be paid for at least in part by an employer, and they attract certain tax breaks.

The disadvantage is that they tend not to be as flexible as other forms of savings when you come to take the benefits.

They have also lost credibility over the years due to mis-selling scandals and the perception that they are somehow risky. Nonetheless they will form at least part of most people's income in retirement and for many the largest part of that income. For this reason it's important that we understand at least some of the basics.

What types of pension exist?

There are many different types of pension, but the good news is that with the exception of the state pension, nearly everyone falls into one of two categories: defined benefit or defined contribution.

The following are examples of defined benefit pensions:

▶ *final salary pensions*
▶ *average salary pensions.*

The following are types of defined contribution pensions:

▶ *Company money purchase pensions*
▶ *Personal pensions (PPP)*
▶ *Self-Employed Retirement Annuity Contracts (SERA): these are also known as Retirement Annuity Contracts (RAC)*
▶ *Free-Standing Additional Voluntary Contributions*
▶ *Group Personal Pensions*
▶ *Stakeholder pensions*
▶ *Executive Pension Plans*
▶ *Small Self-Administered Schemes (SSAS)*
▶ *Self-Invested Pension Plans (SIPP)*
▶ *Company buy-out plans (also known as Section 32s).*

Insight

At this stage, the terms 'defined benefit' and 'defined contribution' are probably meaningless. I apologize for using these technical terms but by doing so I can explain the common characteristics of these two types of scheme rather than say the same thing again for each 'sub species' of pension. Also once you understand these terms you only have to fit your own pension or pensions into one or two 'boxes'.

Defined benefit pensions

A defined benefit pension works by promising you a certain amount of pension, at a certain retirement date, based on your earnings and the number of years that you are a member of the pension scheme.

> ### *Example*
> If you earned a pension of 1/60th of your final salary for each year you were a member of the pension, were a member of the scheme for 20 years and your final salary was £45,000, you could expect a pension of £15,000 a year, i.e.20/60 of £45,000 = £15,000

Insight
Although the term retirement is used, the key determinant of when the pension will be paid is usually age rather then actual retirement. In years past, 99 times out of 100 these two dates would coincide but this is not necessarily the case today.

The amount of pension you will receive is measured by the final benefit that it provides, hence its name. The scheme must provide the pension promised irrespective of the cost. Whilst you may have to contribute, if the pension costs more than expected (for example if you live longer then anticipated), then the scheme must pick up the additional cost.

The most common form of defined benefit pension is a final salary pension, although other versions, such as average salary, also exist and are becoming more common.

ADDED YEARS ADDITIONAL VOLUNTARY CONTRIBUTIONS

You may be able to increase you pension by buying added years. This is relatively common for public sector schemes, but rare for private sector ones. If you buy added years, the amount of pension you receive will be increased by the number of years you buy.

Example

Hanna Green could complete 25 years' service in her
company pension scheme. Based on her salary of £35,000
this would give her a pension of £10,937.50 and a lump sum of
£32,812.50. She bought two additional years which increased
her pension to £11,812.50 and her lump sum to £35,437.50.

Defined contribution pensions

The best way to understand a defined contribution pension is to
think of it in two distinctive parts. The first part is building up a
pot of money by saving and then investing those savings.

How much you build up in that pot will depend on two factors:

▶ *how much is saved*
▶ *how much those savings grow.*

Example

The table below shows the various amounts you could build up
based on different contributions, timescales and growth rates.

Monthly amount saved	For how long	Growth rate	End amount
£250	20 years	5%	£101,864
£250	20 years	6%	£113,911
£275	25 years	7%	£216,554

The second part of a defined contribution pension is using the
savings you have built up to buy an income for life.

How much pension you can buy will depend on a number of
factors including:

▶ *how much you have accumulated*
▶ *how you want to take your pension benefits*
▶ *your age and gender*

- *what pension rates are available at the time*
- *your health.*

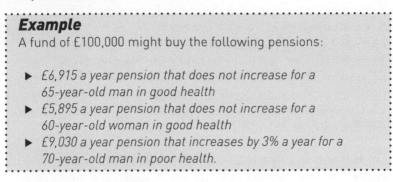

Example

A fund of £100,000 might buy the following pensions:

- *£6,915 a year pension that does not increase for a 65-year-old man in good health*
- *£5,895 a year pension that does not increase for a 60-year-old woman in good health*
- *£9,030 a year pension that increases by 3% a year for a 70-year-old man in poor health.*

INVESTMENT CHOICE

When money is saved into a defined contribution pension it is invested. Some plans will allow you a wide choice of different investments, others no choice at all. As a general rule the more modern a plan the more choice you are likely to have, with many plans now offering a choice of 100 or more different funds.

Along with the amount saved, the amount the fund grows will have an impact on how much you will build up over the years.

One of the benefits of having a choice of funds is that you may be able to transfer to a low-risk fund when approaching retirement.

Insight

If you can do so it is always worth considering transfer to a low-risk fund as you get nearer to retirement in order to protect the savings you have already built up.

Different types of defined contribution pension

Whilst all defined contribution pensions share the same common characteristics, i.e. a savings fund that builds up that is then used to buy a pension, when you take benefits there are differences between them. The section below explains all of the common types.

Personal pensions

A personal pension is one that you take out as an individual although you, your employer or indeed anyone else can pay into the pension. The pension provider will claim basic rate tax relief on contributions you make personally, so if you save £80 the pension provider will claim £20 from the tax man for you, making the total contribution £100.

You will probably have a choice of funds where the money is actually invested but this is not always the case.

Even if your policy document states a specific retirement age, you can take benefits between the ages of 55 and 75, although there may be a penalty if this doesn't coincide with the date you originally selected.

You don't have to take your pension with the company with whom you have saved and you can shop around for a better deal. This is always worth investigating and is explained more fully later in the book.

You can take 25% of your fund as a tax-free lump sum and the rest must be used to buy a pension for life.

Protected Rights and Non-Protected Rights

Your pension may be broken down into Protected Rights and Non-Protected Rights. Protected Rights refers to contributions made as a result of contracting out of the State Earnings-Related Pension (SERPS and/or S2P) and Non-Protected Rights to contributions made by you and your employer.

There are some technical differences between Protected Rights and Non-Protected Rights in terms of the way you can take benefits, the main one being if you are married or in a civil partnership you must take a spouse's pension of at least 50%.

These rules have changed over the years and your policy document may say something different to this, for example it may say that you cannot take any tax-free cash but the changes in the rules override this.

Stakeholder pensions
A stakeholder pension is the same as any other personal pension, the only difference is the charges and conditions are regulated by law.

Self-Employed Retirement Annuities
These were the first type of personal pension that were widely available and ran from 1970 to 1988.

They are also known as Retirement Annuity Contracts and occasionally S226 Plans and despite their name they were also available to employees who were not in a company pension.

They tended to have less choice over where you could invest your money and other differences originally included:

▶ *You could only take benefits between the ages of 60 and 75.*
▶ *There was a different method for calculating how much tax-free cash you could take.*
▶ *You usually had to claim back the tax relief yourself.*

These first two points have now been overridden by new rules that came into force in 2006. Despite what your pension plan documents may say:

▶ *You can take benefits between the ages of 55 and 75.*
▶ *You can take up to 25% of the fund you have built up as a tax-free lump sum (although if the old method meant you could take more than 25% you will usually be allowed to take the higher amount).*

Your pension provider may also collect the tax relief on your behalf. However, not all providers have updated their computer systems to allow this to happen, in which case you will still need to reclaim the tax relief yourself.

Group Personal Pension (GPP)

Group Personal Pensions work in exactly the same way as any other personal pension. The only difference is that they are organized by your employer and, if you require, they will deduct your contributions directly from your pay. Often your employer will also pay into the plan and the charges normally will be lower than you could have secured individually.

Even though the plan has been set up by your employer, it is your plan and if you leave your employer the plan goes with you and you can continue contributing to the plan if you want to.

Additional Voluntary Contributions (AVC) and Free-Standing Additional Voluntary Contributions (FSAVC)

Until 2006, if you were a member of a company pension scheme you were not allowed to take out a personal pension in respect of the same employment. This meant that if you wanted to save more into a pension you had to take out an AVC or FSAVC. Both of these worked in the same way as any other defined contribution pension. The key difference between the two was an AVC was linked to your company pension whilst you could take out a FSAVC with whomever you wished.

Currently the rules for AVCs and FSAVCs are exactly the same as personal pensions:

- ▶ *You can take a 25% lump sum.*
- ▶ *You have to take benefits between the ages of 55 and 75.*
- ▶ *Age not retirement is the trigger for being able to take benefits.*
- ▶ *You can shop around for a pension.*

If you took out your AVC or FSAVC before 2006 your original documentation will show different rules. In particular it will state that you cannot take a lump sum. This has now been overridden. Even if you haven't been sent updated documentation the new rules apply.

Buy-out plans (sometimes known as Section 32s)

A buy-out plan is a plan designed to allow you to transfer money from a previous company pension. In essence it works pretty much in the same way as any other defined contribution although you cannot add any further contributions to it and it may also guarantee a certain minimum return.

Self-Invested Personal Pensions (SIPP)
These work in the same way as any other personal pension but you have a far greater degree of control over where your money is invested. The primary attraction in this regard is that they can be used to buy a business premises in a highly tax efficient way.

They will often also be highly flexible in the way benefits can be taken.

Executive Pension Plans
These plans derive their name from the fact that they were originally targeted at senior executives as a top-up pension and at small business owners. They were subject to the same rules as company pensions even though they usually only had one or two members.

The primary attraction, in theory at least, was that provided you were a member of the pension long enough you could take a greater proportion of the fund built up as a tax-free lump sum. In some cases this could equate to the entire fund.

Since 2006 this is no longer the case and the same 25% lump sum restriction applies, although if you have built up an entitlement to a higher percentage prior to April 2006 you will be able to keep the higher percentage.

If you transfer an Executive Pension Plan you risk losing this right to a higher lump sum so if you have one of these plans you should seek professional advice before taking any action.

Small Self-Administered Schemes (SSAS)
These schemes tended to be sold to directors of small to medium businesses and the principle attraction was that the scheme could buy a commercial property (usually the business premises of the director's firm).

Taking benefits from this type of pension can be highly complex and is outside the scope of this book. Before taking benefits, specialist advice from an independent adviser familiar with dealing with SSAS should be obtained.

Contracted-In and Contracted-Out Group Money Purchase Plans (CIMP and COMP)

A Group Money Purchase Plan is a company pension but, unlike a final salary scheme, the amount of pension you will receive will depend on the same factors as any other defined contribution pension.

The scheme will usually state a Normal Retirement Date (NRD) which is the age at which you can take benefits. Current rules mean you do not have to take benefits on this date but there may be a penalty for taking your pension before this date and no advantage in delaying.

It may also offer favourable terms if you take the pension with the scheme provider, although you do not have to and it still may pay to shop around.

The difference between a COMP and CIMP is that a COMP is also used to contract out of the State Earnings-Related Pension and the fund built up from contracted-out contributions can be separately identified as Protected Rights.

Defined benefit pensions in more detail

WHAT FORMS OF DEFINED BENEFIT PENSION ARE THERE?

The most common form of defined benefit pension is the final salary pension, where benefits are linked to your final salary. In second place, but a long way behind final salary schemes in terms of numbers, are average salary schemes. With an average salary scheme the amount of pension paid is linked to the average of your salary for the time you were a member of the pension scheme, although your salary will usually be adjusted to make at least some allowance for inflation.

The explanations that follow, unless stated, apply to both final salary and average salary schemes.

TAX-FREE CASH FROM DEFINED BENEFIT SCHEMES

Since 2006, the maximum lump sum you can take from a pension is restricted to 25% of the value of your pension fund. As defined benefit pensions do not have an easily identifiable value, there is a formula laid down by HMRC to enable these schemes to give a nominal value on which to base tax-free cash.

Also since 2006, tax-free cash is now technically known as a Pension Commencement Lump Sum (PCLS) and this is the term that will be used on official correspondence. However the expression tax-free cash is still widely used and except in a tiny proportion of cases, the lump sum is still tax free.

Although the maximum lump sum you can take is 25% of the value of your pension fund (as defined by the HMRC formula), in practice most schemes will initially calculate the amount in one of two ways.

Most private sector schemes will allow you to exchange a certain amount of your pension for a lump sum. For example, if you are entitled to a pension of £15,000 a year you take a lower pension of £12,000 in return for a £50,000 lump sum.

Most public sector schemes work the other way around in that they promise a certain amount of lump sum linked to your pensionable salary and the years you have been a member of the pension. Typically you will earn 3/80 of your final salary for each year that you are a member. For example, if your final salary was £45,000 and you had been a member for 20 years you would be entitled to a lump sum of £33,750 (£45,000 × 3/80 × 20 years = £33,750).

This lump sum is in addition to the pension although it will usually be possible to give up some or all of the lump sum to increase the pension.

Either of these methods may result in a lump sum that is higher or lower than the maximum 25% permitted by HMRC. If you were a member of the pension scheme before 2006 you may be allowed to take a higher percentage, but your pension scheme will tell you how much lump sum you can take.

If the lump sum is lower than the 25% allowed, your pension scheme is currently not obliged to give you the option of taking the full 25%, but most will.

Insight

Although most people do take the lump sum, from a purely financial perspective it may not always prove to be best value. The next chapter explores the pros and cons of taking the lump sum along with showing you how to calculate if it is the right thing for you.

PENSIONABLE PAY

Not all of your pay may be pensionable. You may have bonuses or benefits in kind, such as a company car, that don't count towards your pension. Your pension scheme administrator will be able to tell you what your pensionable pay is.

INFLATION

There are two aspects to inflation: firstly, how much your pension increases in line with inflation before you take benefits and secondly how much it increases after you have started to draw your pension.

If your pension is a final salary scheme, then in some respects inflation before retirement is automatically built in. This is because as your salary increases so does your pension. If you have an average salary pension, then the usual position is for your salary to be adjusted to take account of inflation.

With regard to how much your pension will increase in payment will depend on your scheme. Most defined benefit pensions will include some degree of protection against inflation although the detail can be highly complex, particularly if the scheme is a contracted-out one. A contracted-out scheme is one that promises to pay benefits at least equal to the second tier state pension (details on the state pension are given below).

Just to make matters worse, in terms of understanding how much inflation protection you will have, some increases are compulsory and others are discretionary where the trustees of the scheme can choose if and how much your pension will increase, but it is reasonable to assume that most defined benefit pension schemes will give you at least some inflation protection.

SPOUSE'S/DEPENDANTS' PENSION AND DEATH BENEFITS

Most defined benefit pension schemes will continue to pay a pension to your husband or wife if you die before them. They may also pay a pension to any children you have under the age of 23 or who are disabled and dependent on you financially.

The amount of spouse's pension (spouse includes civil partners) that will be paid will usually be expressed as a percentage of your own pension with 50% being a typical amount. If you are single it is unlikely that you will be able to obtain an additional pension even though a spouse's pension will not be paid.

Example

Bill Jarvis has just taken benefits from his pension and after taking his lump sum will have a pension income of £25,000 a year. Unfortunately he dies after a year leaving a widow Jane. The pension provides a 50% spouse's pension, so Jane will receive an income of £12,500 a year for as long as she lives.

WHAT IS THE DEFINITION OF FINAL SALARY?

This section only applies to final salary and not average salary schemes.

What constitutes your final salary varies from scheme to scheme. A common definition is your basic pay plus the average of the final three years' varying income such as bonuses, as shown in the example below.

Example

In the three years before she took benefits from her pension, Jackie West had a basic income of £40,000. She had also received bonuses of:

▶ *£3,000 in the year she retired*
▶ *£5,000 the year before*
▶ *£1,000 the year before that*

These bonuses will be averaged to give her an average bonus of £3,000 which will be added to her basic salary to give her a final salary of £43,000

Insight

This is just one example. Different schemes have different rules and many have several definitions. If this is the case, the one that gives you the most favourable outcome for you will normally be used.

NORMAL RETIREMENT DATE

A defined benefit pension will have something known as a Normal Retirement Date (NRD). This is the date you can take your pension. In the past this date coincided with the date you actually retired and left your employer. However, whilst the term is still used, it now refers to the age at which you become entitled to take benefits from the scheme. Whilst this *may* coincide with the date you retire, the law says you are allowed to draw your pension and continue working either for the same or different employer. Conversely you don't have to draw your pension when you retire.

Whether either of these options will make sense in practice will largely depend on the scheme rules and your personal circumstances. For example, most schemes will impose a penalty if you take benefits before the date set by the scheme and many will not pay you any more if you delay taking benefits.

Example 1

Bill Jarvis is a member of a pension scheme with a Normal Retirement Date of 65. He has now reached this age and wants to continue working and his employer wants him to stay. Whilst Bill doesn't have to take his pension benefits now, his benefits will not increase other than for inflation. Therefore he has decided to continue working and take his pension.

Example 2

Melanie Morris has reached 60 and is retiring from her employer. Her normal scheme retirement date is 65. If she retires and waits until 65 before taking her pension benefits they will pay her a pension of £20,000 a year for life. If she takes the benefits now, the pension will be still be payable for life but it will only pay £15,000 a year.

Insight

There is usually very little choice as to how the benefits will be paid under a defined benefit pension other than whether or not to take a lump sum. It is possible to transfer the pension to another type that offers more choice, but rarely will it pay you to do this.

Contributions to pensions

The rules on how much you can pay into a pension apply to both defined benefit and defined contribution pensions.

You, your employer or indeed anyone else can contribute to your pension on your behalf and the person paying the premium will obtain tax relief. There is no limit on how much can be paid into a pension, but in practice there is a limit for how much an individual can pay and be eligible for tax relief. From 2010 this limit is effectively the lesser of 100% of your earnings or £130,000.

> **Example**
> In the tax year 2008, Bill Wight earned £38,000 so this is the maximum he can pay into his pension and still obtain tax relief.

'Frozen' pensions

Insight

Whilst the term 'frozen' pension is widely used there is actually no such thing. If you leave or stop paying into a pension it should still grow but how it does so depends on the type of scheme. If you are no longer in a pension scheme you are known as a deferred member.

If you leave a defined benefit pension then the amount of pension that you will receive will usually increase between the date of leaving and the Normal Retirement Date of the scheme. The amount of the increase will depend on when you left the scheme and whether or not your pension was contracted out of the earnings-related state pension.

> **Example**
> Nina Page left her employer Humber Ltd in 1999. She had been a member of the final salary pension scheme and had built up a pension of £15,000. In 2009 she reached the age where her pension payments commenced. The actual amount paid was £19,500 a year.

Insight

Very occasionally it will make sense to transfer deferred pension benefits to another type of pension such as a personal pension. However this is very rare and if an adviser suggests you do this then be extremely suspicious as they may be thinking about their commission rather than your best interests.

If you leave or stop paying into a defined contribution pension the funds you have built up to date will stay invested and will rise and fall in line with the actual investment.

> ### Example
> Frank West had a personal pension and had contributed £100 a month before tax relief for 15 years. He stopped paying into the pension ten years ago when he joined a new company that provided a pension for him. When he stopped paying into the pension it was worth £38,345. Ten years later he wants to take benefits from the pension and his plan is worth £68,670.

Insight

The example above assumes a growth rate after charges of 6% a year both during the time Frank was contributing and the time he was not. In practice no pension will produce the same amount of growth year on year. Some years will be higher than others and in all probability in some years the value will fall. However, the percentage fall or rise has nothing to do with whether or not contributions are being made or not.

State pensions

There are three elements to the state pension:

▶ *basic state pension*
▶ *earnings-related pension*
▶ *pension credit.*

> **Insight**
>
> A few months before your state retirement age you will be
> sent a forecast telling you how much state pension you will
> receive. If you want to find out before then the easiest way of
> doing so is to complete a form known as a BR19. Details on
> how to do this can be found at the end of the book.

THE BASIC STATE PENSION

The basic state pension is payable to both those who have been
employed and self-employed. It is calculated weekly but paid every
four weeks.

From April 2010 to receive the full basic state pension you will
need to have paid or received credit for National Insurance
contributions for 30 Years. Prior to this date in order to receive a
full pension, men needed to have paid NI or received credits for
44 years and Women 39 years.

Both men and women will usually receive credits if they are not
working and bringing up children under the age of 16 or are
unemployed. There are also other social security benefits that
provide credits for the basic state pension.

The pension is currently payable at age 65 for men. For women
born on or after 6 April 1950 it will increase gradually to 65
between 2010 and 2020. From 6 April 2020 the state pension age
will be 65 for both men and women.

The easiest way to find out if this increase in retirement age will
apply to you is to visit the Directgov website (www.directgov.co.uk)
and type in state pension age. You will then be taken to a calculator
where you can type in your date of birth and obtain your retirement
date. The BR19 also shows your retirement date.

You can delay taking your state pension for up to five years and
receive an increased pension.

Insight

One of the most common areas of misunderstanding is around what is commonly known as the 'married man's pension'. This pension no longer exists and many couples will each receive a full state pension in their own right. The rules are explained below.

Provided you have paid sufficient National Insurance contributions and/or received sufficient NI credits you will receive a full basic state pension in your own right. For many couples this will mean that they will both receive the full basic state pension.

Example

Tom and Mary are both approaching state retirement age. They are married with two grown-up children. Tom has worked and paid National Insurance contributions for most of his life but has been made redundant a couple of times meaning he hasn't worked for a total of about two years throughout his working life. Mary also worked for 14 years before the children were born but has never gone back to paid employment.

Both will receive a full state pension in their own right as Tom has paid NI contributions for more than 30 years. Mary will have 14 years' National Insurance contributions and will receive credits for the years her children were under 16 meaning she also will be entitled to a full basic state pension.

If you haven't paid sufficient NI contributions or received sufficient credit but your husband, wife or civil partner has, then you will be able to claim a state pension based on their NI record when you reach state retirement age. Under present rules this will a pension equal to 60% of your spouse's or civil partner's pension.

Insight

Up until 1977 a married woman could pay a reduced rate of National Insurance commonly known as 'the married woman's stamp'. If this applies to you then the rules above will apply to you also.

Example

Jane is approaching 60 and hasn't worked since she married
Angus when they where both aged 20. Jane will be able to
claim a state pension when she reaches age 60 because
Angus has paid NI contributions for more than 30 years.
Jane's pension will be 60% of a single person's pension but
Angus will not be able to draw his pension until he is 65. When
he is 65 Angus will be able to draw his state pension and Jane
will continue to receive a state pension in her own right.

These rules changed in April 2010. Before that date to claim this
additional pension your spouse or civil partner had to have reached
state retirement age and started drawing their state pension.

Insight

Many people, including retirement planners, choose to ignore
the state pension as insignificant but this is a mistake. At the
time of writing the combined state pension for a couple who
are both entitled to a basic state pension amounts to around
£10,000 a year. Whilst this is not very much it does form a
stable guaranteed income on which to build the rest of your
retirement planning.

EARNINGS-RELATED PENSION

With the exception of a three-year gap between 1975 and 1978
some form of earnings-related state pension has existed for
employees since 1961. Over this time there have been three
versions:

- *1961–75: Graduated Pension Scheme*
- *1978–2002: State Earnings-Related Pension Scheme (SERPS)*
- *2002–present: Second State Pension (S2P)*

All of them share the feature that the amount of pension paid
is linked to your earnings although the rates vary between the
different versions.

Exploring the technicalities of how each of these three versions of earnings-related pension work is not really required but all of them:

▶ *will have the amount shown on a state pension forecast*
▶ *in the main only apply to employees*
▶ *will not take all of your earnings into account*
▶ *will be paid in addition to your basic state pension*
▶ *except the Graduated Scheme allow you to contract out of the earnings-related pension.*

A more detailed explanation of each of these points is given below.

The amount you will receive will be shown on a state pension forecast

When you receive a state pension forecast it will show:

▶ *the amount of basic state pension you will receive*
▶ *the amount, if any, of Graduated Pension you will receive*
▶ *the amount, if any, of SERPS pension you will receive*
▶ *the amount, if any, of S₂P pension you will receive.*

The forecast will show the amount in today's money, so the actual amount you will receive will probably be more than is shown on the forecast but it will only be worth the amount shown.

Example

Hanna Richards is retiring this month. A year ago she obtained a state pension forecast which showed she was entitled to a basic state pension of £92.25 a week and earnings-related benefits of £45.66 making her total state pension £140.91 a week or £7,327.32 a year. When she actually receives her pension she receives £147.96 a week. This is because in the last year inflation has been 5%, so the amount of her pension has also gone up by this amount. However her cost of living has also increased, meaning that £147.96 a week will only buy her what £140.91 a week did last year.

In the main they only apply to employees

Earnings-related pensions are not available to the self-employed although if you have been self-employed for some of your working life and employed for some, unless you were in a contracted-out pension you will probably have an earnings-related pension for those years that you were employed.

Example

Fred Jackson started working for Smiths Engineers when he was 16. He worked for them until he was 36 and was then self-employed until he retired and drew his state pension at the age of 65. He will receive his basic state pension based on all of his working life and an additional earnings-related pension for the years of 16 to 36.

Not all your earnings are taken into account

Your earnings-related pension is calculated on what is known as band earnings. What this means is that earnings above and below a certain level are ignored. These bands are different for each of the three types of scheme and are adjusted each year.

They are paid in addition to your basic state pension

Any earnings-related pension you have will be paid in addition to your basic state pension and they start at the same age. They must start at the same time as you cannot ask for your basic state pension to be paid and delay taking the earnings-related pension or vice versa.

You can contract out of the State Earnings-Related Pension Scheme

Insight

Nearly everyone has heard of contracting out but not everyone knows what it means. Contracting out means your company or personal pension scheme will pay you a pension instead of the government. You can only contract out of the earnings-related (i.e. not basic) state pension and it works differently for defined benefit and defined contribution pensions.

You have been able to contract out of the earnings-related pensions using a defined benefit scheme since 1978, and since 1988 for a defined contribution scheme including personal pensions. This means you will not receive an earnings-related pension from the state in respect of those years you have been contracted out. Instead you will receive a pension from your company or personal pension.

If you have a defined benefit pension such as a final salary scheme, the whole scheme will be contracted out, and if you are a member you will not have any choice in the matter. You will also be contracted out for as long as you are a member of that scheme.

Most final salary schemes are contracted out, although they don't have to be and you will probably not receive a higher pension as a result. Whilst on one level this may seem unfair you will have received a reduction in your National Insurance contributions for each and every year that you have been a member of the contracted-out scheme, although you have probably never been told this.

Example

Paul Smith works for ABC Ltd and earns £30,000 a year. He is a member of the ABC contracted-out final salary pension and takes home £1,917.68 a month. He leaves ABC Ltd and goes to work for XYZ Ltd for exactly the same salary of £30,000 a year but only takes home £1,885.30. This £32.38 a month difference is entirely due to the difference in National Insurance contributions for someone who is a member of a defined benefit contracted-out pension scheme and someone who is not.

Contracting out through a defined contribution pension works in a slightly different way and it will come as no surprise to learn that even this subdivides in two categories: one for defined contribution company pensions and one for personal pensions.

For personal pensions you still pay the same rate of National Insurance but, for each year you are contracted out, some of those contributions are redirected to a pension of your choice. That money is then invested and the amount of pension you will receive is largely determined by how much that money will grow. The contracted-out pension can be separately identified from any other pension you have built up through your own contributions as it is called Protected Rights.

The decision to contract out or indeed to contract back into the earnings-related state pension is an annual one. You could contract out one year, contract back in the next and out again the following. How this works in practice is that once you have arranged to be contracted out that decision will automatically be renewed every year until you tell you pension provider that you no longer want to.

Insight

I am often asked by clients if they should contract out of the earnings-related state pension, or if they are already contracted out should they contract back in. The answer to this question will depend on a number of factors including your attitude to investment risk, marital status, and the age at which you intend to take benefits. That being said contracting out using a personal pension is being abolished in 2012 so you may feel the easiest answer is to just carry on as you are now.

Pension credits

Insight

Official statistics show that up to two out of five people entitled to pension credit are not claiming it. I assume there are a number of reasons for this.

- ▶ *People simply do not know that it exists.*
- ▶ *The process for claiming it can be complex.*
- ▶ *Many people underestimate how much income and/or savings they can have in order to claim.*

I therefore urge you to read this section and, if you are in the slightest doubt as to whether or not you are eligible, make enquiries to see if you are.

Nearly every UK resident is entitled to a minimum amount of income when they reach the age of 60. If they have some savings this amount is increased when they reach age 65.

Both income and savings are taken into account when assessing whether or not you are eligible, but the level of savings in some case can be over £60,000.

There are two parts to pension credit:

▶ *guaranteed credit*
▶ *savings credit*

Guaranteed credit

Guaranteed credit is available from age 60 and you can apply for pension credit irrespective of whether you are working or not. Unlike other state pensions the age of 60 applies to both men and women. For a couple it is the age of the elder that is used.

Savings credit

If you are over the age of 65 you may be entitled to savings credit. Once again the age limit applies to men and women and in the case of a couple only the elder has to be this age.

The rules are incredibly complex but the concept is that if you are over the age of 65 you can have a higher income and/or savings than at 60 and be entitled to some credit.

Insight

Whilst working out how much pension credit you may be entitled to is highly complex, but the good news is that you don't have to. On the Directgov website (www.directgov.co.uk) you will find a calculator where you can enter your personal details and find out if you are entitled to pension credit. Alternatively, a phone number is given at the end of this book and you can call for an estimate.

TEN POINTS TO REMEMBER

1 *Nearly every type of pension except state pensions fall into one of two categories: defined benefit or defined contribution.*

2 *The amount of pension you receive from a defined benefit scheme is based on the years you have been a scheme member and your salary.*

3 *The amount of pension you will receive from a defined contribution pension will largely depend on:*
 ▷ *the amount paid in*
 ▷ *how much that amount grows*
 ▷ *how much pension you can buy with that money.*

4 *Other than whether or not to take a lump sum, you have a limited number of choices about how to take benefits under a defined benefit scheme.*

5 *With a defined contribution scheme you will usually have a choice over where your money is actually invested and how to take benefits.*

6 *There is no such thing as a frozen pension, only deferred pensions.*

7 *There are two parts to the state pension: the basic state pension and an earnings-related part.*

8 *To obtain the maximum basic state pension you will have needed to have paid National Insurance contributions or received credits for 30 years.*

9 *You can obtain a state pension forecast by completing a BR19 form.*

10 *As well as the state pension, the state provides a safety net minimum income known as pension credit.*

5

Pension choices: part 1

In this chapter you will:
- *consider the implications of delaying your pension*
- *think about the pros and cons of taking a lump sum*

Insight

As mentioned already, when you come to take benefits from your pension you will be faced with a number of choices. The amount of choice you will have will depend on the type of pension you have, with defined benefit schemes having less choice than defined contribution ones. The most important point is that whatever type of scheme you have, most of the decisions you make will be irreversible and will stay with you for the rest of your life.

The table on page 74 indicates the choices that are *likely* to be available under different types of pension, but remember each pension is different so you will need to check with your employer or pension company to see if they apply to you.

Even if a particular choice is not available to you, you will usually have the right to transfer to a pension that does have the particular option you require. This may not always be a good idea and will require specialist advice.

Ideally these points should be considered some time before you actually want or need to take the pension, as it will help you to know what action, if any, you may want to take. For

Choice	Defined benefit pension	Defined contribution occupational scheme	Personal pension
Ability to delay taking pension	Possible	Probable	Yes
Take tax-free lump sum	Yes	Yes	Yes
Take a pension that will continue to be paid to a spouse and/or dependants' pension if you die before them	Scheme rules will dictate if payable or not and amount	Yes	Yes
Choice of a pension that will increase every year or stay at the same amount	Scheme rules will dictate amount of increase (if any)	Probably	Yes
A lump sum payable on death before age 75	Unlikely	Possible	Yes
Ability to take all the pension as a lump sum	Dependent on your health or amount of pension fund	Dependent on your health or amount of pension fund	Dependent on your health or amount of pension fund
Ability to shop around for higher pension	Theoretically yes, but unlikely to achieve a higher pension	Yes	Yes
A guaranteed or variable pension	Unlikely	Unlikely	Yes

example, if you are married you may need to decide whether or not you should take a pension for your husband or wife if you die before them. Some pensions will pay less if you want to take this option. Therefore, knowing how much you can expect from both options is important to help you plan which will be best for you.

Should you take your pension?

In this section we will consider:

▶ *why someone may want to delay taking a pension*
▶ *the pros and cons of delaying taking your pension.*

Previously we discussed whether you might want to delay taking your pension. As a reminder, the reasons for this were that you may not need the money yet and:

▶ *the pension may increase if you don't take it immediately*
▶ *the pension will be added to any other income you have and you will probably have to pay tax on it.*

Insight

If you don't need to take your pension at the date it was originally set up, you will need to weigh up whether you will be better off by delaying. Whether this is worth even considering will depend on what will happen to your pension if you delay. There are three possibilities; your pension:

▶ *will not increase*
▶ *will definitely increase*
▶ *may increase or decrease.*

The first thing to do therefore is ask your pension provider which of these three options apply to your existing pension. Once you know this, you can decide what your next step will be.

PENSIONS THAT WILL DEFINITELY NOT INCREASE

In this situation your choice is clear as there is no advantage in delaying taking benefits. You may as well take the pension immediately.

PENSIONS THAT WILL DEFINITELY INCREASE

If you have a pension that will definitely increase you will need to weigh up the amount of the increase against the amount you will have lost by not taking the pension immediately.

Example

Jenny Jackson was a member of a defined benefit pension scheme with a retirement age of 60. If she took the pension at 60 it would pay her a pension of £10,000 and a lump sum of £30,000. Each year she delayed, the pension and lump sum would increase by 8%. By delaying for a year her pension increased to £10,800 a year and the lump sum to £32,400.

On the surface it would make sense for Jenny to delay taking her pension, provided of course she didn't need the income. However there is one more calculation she needs to carry out and that is to take into account the fact that she has not received the pension for a year. For simplicity if we ignore tax and any inflation increases in pension and interest she would have received on the lump sum the calculation is:

1 Calculate the additional lump sum if she delays. £2,400

2 Calculate the additional annual pension. £800 a year

3 Calculate how much pension she will lose by not having pension paid immediately. £10,000

4 Deduct additional lump sum from the figure in 3. £10,000 – £2,400 = £7,600

5 Divide the answer in 4 by the increased pension. £7,600 ÷ £800 = 9.5

Based on this it will take Jenny 9½ years for the extra £800 to make up the loss of one year's pension income. If the pension increased each year and tax was taken into account then the 9½ years would probably reduce a little further.

PENSIONS THAT MAY INCREASE OR DECREASE

This will apply to defined contribution schemes including personal pensions because, until you actually take your pension, your money is still invested and that investment could rise or fall in value. Whether it could fall and by how much will depend on where that money is invested.

If you are considering delaying taking the benefits from a defined contribution pension the first thing to find out is where your money is actually invested and how likely it is to fall in value. Unless there is very little chance of this happening you will need to carefully consider if you are prepared to risk this.

It may be possible to move your pension to a fund that will not or is less likely to fall in value. Examples of this include cash and deposit funds, although before moving funds you should ask your provider if you will lose any guaranteed benefits by doing so.

Insight

Providing there is no penalty for doing so, if you can it usually makes sense in the run-up to retirement to transfer to a low-risk fund to protect the amount you have built up in the pension.

Even if your pension is invested in a fund that is unlikely to fall in value there are still a couple of points you need to take into account:

▶ *the risk that pension rates could fall*
▶ *how much income you will lose by not taking benefits.*

THE RISK THAT PENSION RATES COULD FALL

At any one point in time the older you are the more income you will be able to buy with the pot of money you have accumulated. However, pension rates frequently change. If you delay taking your pension you run the risk that pension rates could fall, meaning the amount of pension you could buy could be reduced. On the other hand, rates could increase meaning an even higher pension.

Insight

Whilst it may be possible to make an educated guess, no one can be absolutely certain as to whether rates will fall or rise.

HOW MUCH INCOME YOU WILL LOSE BY NOT TAKING BENEFITS

This is the same issue as discussed above (see 'Should you take your pension?'), i.e. you will need to weigh up how much extra income you may receive in the future against what you will lose by not taking benefits immediately. However, unlike the situation where you know how much extra pension you will obtain by delaying, in this case you are foregoing a certain income for the possibility of an increased pension in the future.

Insight

Because of this complexity, I am sometimes asked by clients to prepare a report setting out the pros and cons of taking benefits immediately against delaying them. Whilst we can make some assumptions about likely increases, more often than not the decision is based on whether they would prefer the certainty of taking their pension straight away or the possibility of it increasing if they delay.

SPECIAL RULES – PUBLIC SECTOR AND SOME OTHER PENSIONS

If you are a member of a public sector pension and continue to work for the same organization beyond your Normal Retirement

Date (NRD) and draw your pension, in some circumstances your pension will be reduced until you stop working or your earnings fall below a certain level.

If you are intending to work for the same organization after your Normal Retirement Date and draw your pension, you will need to check with your pensions administrator if this will impact on you.

Should you take the tax-free lump sum?

In this section we will consider:

▶ *the rules on taking a lump sum from a pension*
▶ *the pros and cons of taking the lump sum*
▶ *ways of generating an income from the pension lump sum*
▶ *taking all of your pension as a lump sum.*

Insight

The tax-free lump sum from a pension is one of its main attractions. Thousands of pensions have been arranged on the promise of a Caribbean cruise or 'the car you have always dreamed of'. Taking the lump sum will always mean reducing your ongoing pension income and from a purely financial basis that doesn't always make sense.

Even if it doesn't always make the most sense from a financial perspective, it doesn't mean to say that you shouldn't take the lump sum' – most people do. It may well be that the tax-free cash you receive will help you realize a lifelong dream or just enable you to buy a few things that you have been promising yourself for years. Alternatively you may want to use the lump sum for a specific purpose such as to pay off your mortgage or buy a property overseas.

The lump sum you can take from a pension is now known as the Pension Commencement Lump Sum (you will often see this referred to as PCLS) although many people still refer to it as tax-free cash.

The considerations as to whether or not to take it are slightly different for defined contribution and defined benefit pensions. From a purely financial perspective, generally speaking, taking the lump sum:

▶ *will often be poor value for defined benefit pensions*
▶ *will be neutral for defined contribution pensions.*

TAKING THE LUMP SUM FROM A DEFINED BENEFIT PENSION

With a defined benefit pension you have to give up some of your pension in order to take a lump sum. Some pensions, for example most public sector schemes, work the other way round and you can give up the lump sum to buy extra pension. Either way the effect is the same: if you take the lump sum you will have a lower pension.

In working out if taking the lump sum is good value or not you have to compare the amount of pension you have to give up with the amount of lump sum you will obtain.

Example

Pam is 60 and about to receive benefits from her company pension and has been sent details of her pension as follows:

full pension	£16,941 a year
lump sum	£75,118
reduced pension	£11,367 a year

This means that to take the maximum lump sum from the pension she has to give up £5,674 a year pension.

The simplest way of working out if taking the lump sum is good value or not is to divide it by the amount of pension lost to see how many years it would last. In this case the figure would be just over 13 years. If Pam lives more than 13 years she will be worse off taking the lump sum. If she lives less that than 13 years she would be better off.

This method is not entirely accurate as it ignores a number of factors. These include the impact of tax, the fact that the pension will increase every year and she could invest the lump sum, but for our purpose it is probably as good as any other more sophisticated method.

> **Insight**
>
> In this instance taking the lump sum doesn't really represent very good value as Pam is only 60 and would expect to live a lot longer than 13 years.

Other points to consider – defined benefit schemes

Firstly, some defined benefit schemes, particularly public sector schemes, calculate the lump sum in a different way. Rather than giving up pension to buy the lump sum it is shown as a separate amount based on your final salary and the years you have worked for the organization. You can convert this lump sum to a pension and the same considerations apply as if you have to convert your pension to a lump sum.

However, the basic lump sum often works out to be less than the 25% permitted by HMRC and as such many of these schemes will allow you to increase the lump sum by giving up some pension. The important point here is that the rate of conversion can be different for converting the lump sum to pension than pension to lump sum. What this means is that whilst it can make sense to take the basic lump sum it will often not be worthwhile taking the increased amount.

Secondly, if you have a defined benefit pension it will probably have a spouse's pension that will pay an income to your husband or wife for the rest of their life if you should die before them. Taking the lump sum could reduce this as well and this is a point you should consider if you intend to buy an income with the lump sum.

Thirdly, some defined benefit pension schemes, particularly public sector schemes have very generous provision for inflation. Whilst it is possible to defend yourself against inflation to a certain degree, if high levels of inflation were to return for any extended period your standard of living could be seriously affected.

TAKING THE LUMP SUM FROM A DEFINED CONTRIBUTION PENSION

With a defined contribution pension, because there is a clearly identified fund value and you don't have to convert income to a lump sum or vice versa, things are much more straightforward.

Your pension will still be reduced but it will usually be on a £ for £ basis. Thus, if you had a fund of £100,000 that would buy a pension of £10,000 a year; £75,000 would buy a pension of £7,500 a year.

In fact, due to the way pensions are taxed it can pay you to take the lump sum and buy an annuity with it. This is explained below.

Using the lump sum to generate income

If you want to use the lump sum to generate an income you basically have two choices:

- *buy an income for life with it (an annuity)*
- *invest it and use the interest or capital to boost your income.*

In either case you will have to compare how much income you can generate with the lump sum with the income you have to give up from the pension.

BUYING AN INCOME FOR LIFE (AN ANNUITY)

One of the choices you have with your tax-free lump sum is to buy an income for life. This is known as an annuity and it works in the same way as a pension in that it will continue to pay a regular income as long as you live, whether that is for a day or until you are 150 years old.

Insight

Many people are put off annuities because they fear that if they die soon after taking the annuity, their dependants will miss out as the income will stop on their death and they will have effectively 'lost' a large part of their money. These fears are often unfounded as there are annuities available that get around this problem by having some level of capital protection in the event of early death.

If you have a defined benefit pension you will nearly always be better off taking the increased pension from your scheme rather than taking the lump sum and buying an annuity.

If you have a defined contribution pension you may well be able to increase your income by taking the lump sum and using it to buy an annuity.

The annuity you buy with your own money, even if the source of that money is the lump sum from a pension, is known as a Purchased Life Annuity (PLA) and because it is taxed differently you may be able to obtain a higher income £ for £ with this type of annuity than one you *have* to buy from your pension pot.

A pension annuity, or as it is technically known, a Compulsory Purchase Annuity (CPA) is subject to tax on all of the income you receive from it. Only part of a Purchased Life Annuity is subject to tax. This is because HMRC treat part of income generated by a PLA as a return of your capital and this is not taxed.

Example – Pension Annuity v Purchased Life Annuity

Bill is 63 years old and has a pension fund of £250,000. He can use all of this money to buy a pension of £18,480 a year before tax. Alternatively he can take the 25% tax-free lump sum, have a reduced pension of £13,860 and use the lump sum of £62,500 to buy an annuity. Assuming this was Bill's only income the figures could be as follows.

(Contd)

Option 1: take all as pension
Income before tax:

	from pension	£18,480

Income after tax:

	from pension	£16,343

Option 2: use tax-free lump sum to buy annuity
Income before tax:

	from pension	£13,860
	from annuity	£4,620
	total	£18,480

Income after tax:

	from pension	£12,739
	from annuity	£4,321
	total	£17,060

So, on the face of it, Bill is better off by £717 a year or nearly £60 a month, if he uses the tax-free lump sum to buy an annuity. However, there are some additional considerations to take into account.

Firstly, it is essential to compare like for like. The example given assumes that both Bill's pension and his annuity are on a level basis and will not increase every year. It also assumes that the gross income that can be bought will be the same for a pension annuity and a Purchased Life Annuity.

If Bill's pension increased every year whereas the Purchased Life Annuity did not, then the PLA would always look more attractive, but over a period of years the increasing pension would catch up and eventually overtake the PLA.

Secondly, even before tax, the income that can be secured from a Purchased Life Annuity may be different to that which can be obtained from a pension annuity and this may well be lower. For example, Bill may have only been able to buy a gross Purchased Life Annuity of £3,800 compared with the £4,620 he gave up in pension.

This is because statistics show that people who buy Purchased Life Annuities tend to live longer on average than those who buy pension annuities. The annuity will then have to be paid for a longer period and so to compensate, the income will be lower.

Investing in an annuity is covered in more detail in a later chapters.

USING THE LUMP SUM TO INVEST

A more popular choice than an annuity is to invest the lump sum and use the interest and possibly some of the capital to boost income. This option also allows you to invest for capital growth if you do not have an immediate need for the income.

The principle advantages of investing the lump sum are:

▶ **Flexibility:** *you have the lump sum to use as you wish. For example, if you want to draw some money to go on holiday you can; if you want to draw less income in one year than another you can.*
▶ **Control:** *if you buy an annuity or take all of your money as pension, you no longer have the capital. Even if you purchase a capital protected annuity you still lose control of the money.*
▶ **Investment choice:** *you have complete choice over where the money is invested, from very conservative to highly speculative. You can even use the lump sum to buy an annuity at a later stage, but not vice versa.*

The disadvantages are:

▶ **Interest rates:** *may not be high enough to generate sufficient income. Even if they are high enough to generate the income you need initially, they could fall leaving you with insufficient income to meet your requirements.*
▶ **Money could run out:** *if you eat into your capital there is the risk your money could run out before you die.*
▶ **Investments could fall:** *if you place your money in a deposit account over the longer term it will struggle to keep up*

with inflation. Whilst there are some exceptions, most other investments will rise and fall over a period of time.

Example 1 – Investing tax-free lump sum v taking a pension income

Sally is retiring and she has £250,000 built up in her pension fund.

She has been given the following figures to decide if she wants to take the tax-free lump sum or an increased pension:

▶ *a level pension of £16,110 a year*
▶ *tax-free lump sum of £62,500 and a level pension of £12,085 a year.*

In other words, she has to give up an income of £4,025 a year to obtain the tax-free lump sum. She doesn't want to buy an annuity with the lump sum, as she would rather keep control over her money.

To replace the income she has given up from the pension she would need to obtain an interest rate of 6.44% a year. History would suggest that this interest rate is achievable over the longer term but would involve her in taking some investment risk.

However, this example ignores one major factor. If she takes the lump sum, Sally still has that capital, whereas if she has taken the pension she wouldn't. To truly compare like for like we would need to assume that as well as drawing interest Sally would erode the capital at a rate so that there was nothing left on the day she died.

Obviously this is impossible to calculate and highlights one of the benefits of both a pension annuity and Purchased Life Annuity, in that the income cannot run out whilst you are still alive.

However, we can make some reasonable assumptions about how long that money would last. The table below shows how long Sally's capital would last at varying interest rates assuming she drew the same £4,025 a year she has given up in pension income.

Interest rate	How long money would last
1%	16 years
2%	18 years
3%	21 years
4%	24 years
5%	30 years

Therefore if Sally was willing to eat into her capital and expected to live for 24 years, then she would only need to obtain an interest rate of 4%. Faced with this information Sally may well decide she would rather have the lump sum, especially if she feels she would be more active and therefore require more income in the earlier years of retirement.

Example 2 – Investing tax-free lump sum v taking a pension income

Robert is retiring at 60 and his employer has given him the following choices:

► *a pension of £18,000 a year that increases in line with inflation*
► *a lump sum of £40,500 and a pension of £14,800 a year that increases in line with inflation.*

He needs all of the £18,000 to support his desired lifestyle.

This would mean that, even ignoring inflation to match the pension with income generated by investing the lump sum Robert would need to obtain a return of nearly 8% a year. Taking into account inflation, he would need to earn 10%–12%. The only way he could do this would be to take a speculative investment and even then there is no guarantee he would obtain his desired return.

However, Robert is only 60 and whilst he needs all of his income to support his lifestyle, in five years time he will be eligible for his state pension. Also, when he gets to 65 the amount of income he can receive before he pays tax will increase.

Therefore even if he took the lower pension of £14,800 a year, when he was 65 his total income would be higher than he needed to maintain his standard of living.

This doesn't change the fundamental point that he will still need fairly spectacular investment returns from the invested lump sum to match what he has given up in pension, but he may decide that as in five years time he will have enough income to meet his needs, he would rather have the lump sum even if that means eroding his capital for the first five years.

Insight

Where you expect to have an increased income at some stage in the future or receive a lump sum, for example from another pension or from starting or receiving an inheritance, you may consider that eating into your capital is worthwhile.

Small pension funds

If you are between the ages of 60 and 75 and the value of all of your pension funds added together is below a certain limit, then you can take the entire amount as a lump sum. This limit is known as the Triviality Limit and until at least 2016 it is set at £18,000.

25% of the amount you receive is tax free with the balance being subject to tax. Whether you actually pay any tax and the amount you may have to pay will depend on your income in the year you take the pension.

It doesn't matter how many different pensions you have, the limit is the total value of them all put together. For example, you may have three existing pensions with the following values:

Company Pension	£6,758
Personal Pension 1	£3,457
Personal Pension 2	£4,598
Total	£14,813.00

In this case it will be possible to take all of the pensions as a lump sum, as the total value is below the Triviality Limit.

If the value of all your pensions exceeds the Triviality Limit even by a single penny, then you cannot take the whole fund as a lump sum from any of them.

A point to note is that if you have several pensions and one or more is below the Triviality Limit, you will probably get a letter from the pension provider asking whether or not you want to take all of the pension as a lump sum and asking you to confirm that you are eligible to do so. This is because in most cases that provider does not even know if you have another pension, let alone the value.

Whilst it may be tempting not to admit to other pensions and take all the cash, HMRC are notified of *all* pension transactions such as this, and not being completely truthful could result in serious consequences.

Serious ill health

If you are in serious ill health then you will usually be able to take all of your pension as a lump sum and this is not subject to tax provided the value does not exceed £1.8 million.

In order to qualify for a pension to be paid on the grounds of serious ill health, your life expectancy must be less than 12 months and a suitably qualified doctor must certify this.

The exception to being able to take all of your pension as a lump sum in these circumstances is when the pension has been built up as a result of contracting out of the second tier state pension scheme. In this case you will only be able to take all of the fund as a lump sum if you are not married or in a civil partnership. If you fall into one of these categories you will only be able to take half of your fund in respect of contracted-out benefits as a lump sum. The rest will be paid as a pension to you that will continue to paid to your spouse retained after your death.

Example

Shelia is married and has been diagnosed with terminal cancer. Her doctor has confirmed that she expects Shelia has less than a year to live. Shelia's total pensions are worth £56,000 made up as follows.

Source	Amount
From her own contributions	£8,000
From her employer's contributions	£32,000
From contracting out	£16,000

She will be able to take £48,000 as a lump sum and £8,000 must be used to buy a pension for her husband after she has died.

TEN POINTS TO REMEMBER

1 *Taking a lump sum from a pension does not always make financial sense, especially if you want to use it to generate an income.*

2 *You should always ascertain how much pension you will have to forgo in order to take the lump sum from a pension.*

3 *If you want to use the lump sum to increase your income then you basically have two choices:*
   ▷ *buy an annuity*
   ▷ *invest the lump sum.*

4 *The principle advantage of an annuity is that the income cannot run out and will continue until you die.*

5 *The principle disadvantage of the annuity is that you give up capital to buy it.*

6 *The principle advantage of investing the money is that you retain control of your capital.*

7 *The principle disadvantage is that to match the income you could receive from an annuity you may have to draw on the capital.*

8 *Make sure you take into account any provision your existing pension makes for inflation and spouse's pension in order to compare like for like.*

9 *If you need a spouse's pension, make sure any alternative also takes this into account.*

10 *If your life expectancy is less than a year or the value of all of your pensions are under £18,000, then you can take all of your pension as a lump sum.*

6

Pension choices: part 2

In this chapter you will:
- *learn about defined contribution pensions in more detail*
- *learn about annuities and drawdown*
- *work out what choices are best for you*

Defined contribution pensions

If you have a defined contribution pension, then as well as deciding to take or delay your pension and whether or not to take the lump sum you may also have the following choices:

- ▶ *to buy an annuity or draw directly from your pension fund*
- ▶ *a pension that stays at the same amount each year or increases either by fixed amount or in line with inflation*
- ▶ *a pension that will stop when you die, or continue to be paid to your husband, wife or other dependant if you die before them*
- ▶ *a pension that will continue to be paid for a certain number of years if you die shortly after taking it out*
- ▶ *a pension that is paid in advance or arrears*
- ▶ *a pension that will return a lump sum if you die before the age of 75.*

Even if you don't have these choices you will have the ability to move your pension to another provider who does provide these options.

These choices are not mutually exclusive and you could be faced with having to make a decision about many of them at the same time, which can be extremely confusing. To make matters worse, once most of these choices have been made they cannot be reversed and will affect you for the rest of your life, so it is vitally important to get them right from the outset.

Also it is possible to have more than one type of pension so you may have a different range of choices for each pension you hold.

Insight

To help you manage the choices you face it may help to refer back to the answers you gave to the questions in Chapter 2. There is also a table at the end of this chapter that should help you put the flesh on the bones of your original thoughts.

Buy an annuity or draw directly from your pension

Many years ago the only choice you had when taking the benefits from a defined contribution pension was to buy an annuity. An annuity is an income that is guaranteed for life. You now don't have to buy an annuity and there are a number of different options, although in practice the main alternative is something known as drawdown.

As most people will buy an annuity rather than take drawdown, we will consider first the various choices you have when buying an annuity before we move on to drawdown.

A level or increasing pension

You will usually be able to select a pension that increases every year or one that pays more initially but will not increase. The advantage of the former is that you will have some degree of protection against inflation.

Choices for the amount of increase are typically 3%, 5% or Retail Prices Index (RPI). If you choose the RPI option your pension will go up each year in line with the RPI, which is a measure of inflation. However the pension provider will nearly always place a ceiling on the amount of increase they will pay. For example, if a ceiling was set at 5% and RPI went up by 2%, your pension would increase by 2%. If it went up by 5% you would get 5%, but if it went up by 6% your pension would only increase by 5%.

Example
Andrea Kline is 65 and has a pension fund of £100,000. She has the choice of taking a pension that doesn't increase of £6,540 a year, or £4,609 a year for one that increases by 3% a year. It will take about 12 years for the increasing pension to catch up with the level pension and about 22 years for the total amount paid from the increasing pension to exceed the amount paid from the level pension.

Insight
To enable clients to make this choice I always get quotes for a level pension and one that increases by 3% a year. It generally takes 12–14 years for the increasing pension to catch up with the level one, although it does depend on a person's age; the younger they are the longer it takes to catch up. I find most people would rather have the greater income earlier in retirement and so choose a level pension.

A pension that stops when you die or continues to pay to your spouse/dependant
Any pension fund that has been built up through contracting out (this is known as Protected Rights) must include a spouse's pension of at least 50% if you are married or in a civil partnership. For the non-contracted-out part of the pension (known as Non-Protected Rights), you can choose the amount of pension that will continue to be paid to your husband or wife if you die before them. Most providers will allow you to choose any figure between 1% and 200% of your pension.

A dependants' pension can be paid for children up to a maximum age of 23, unless your child is financially dependent on you due to disability, in which case there is no age limit.

Example

Mike Walters is 65 and his wife is 60. He has a pension fund of £100,000 which will buy him a level pension of:

▶ *£6,915 a year if he buys a pension that stops on his death*
▶ *£6,180 a year if the pension continues to pay 50% to his wife if he dies before her*
▶ *£5,566 a year if the pension continues to pay 100% to his wife if he dies before her.*

Insight

The difference between the amount a single life and spouse's pension will pay is partially dependent on the age difference between the couple, whether the spouse's pension will be paid to the husband or wife and their state of health. I find that where a spouse's pension is required, 50% is the most popular option.

With-Profits Annuity

A variation on the increasing pension is what is known as a With-Profits Annuity. With this you select an Anticipated Bonus Rate (ABR), typically between 0% and 5%. The higher the bonus rate you select the higher your starting pension will be.

Every year the insurer will declare if they will pay a bonus and how much. If the bonus is higher than the amount you have selected then your pension will go up. If it is lower it will go down but it can never fall below a minimum level.

Example

Rita Shah has taken out a With-Profits Annuity and elected an ABR of 2%. This will give her a starting income of £5,940 a year. If in a year's time her annuity provider declares a bonus of 2%, her pension will stay the same. If they declare a higher bonus rate it will increase, and if they declare a lower rate it will fall, but never below the guaranteed minimum of £4,709 a year.

Insight

On the surface a With-Profits Annuity appears an attractive option as you know the minimum level of pension you will receive and have the potential for the pension to increase. However, I find that in practice when clients see the figures they don't think the risk of having the pension reduce is one worth taking. For example, if Rita had taken a level guaranteed premium then she would receive an income of £6,455 a year. Also, I must confess a dislike of with profits plans as you are dependent on the annuity provider declaring a bonus.

A pension that continues to be paid for a certain number of years if you die shortly after taking it out

It is possible for the pension to be paid out for a certain minimum number of years, typically five or ten, from the date that it started. This means that if you die shortly after taking the pension it will continue to be paid for the guaranteed period. If you have selected a spouse's pension of less than 100%, the full amount will be paid for the agreed period before reverting to the spouse's percentage.

Example

Alyson Pilch took out a pension that paid her £10,000 a year, and would continue to pay her husband Keith 50%, i.e. £5,000 a year for the rest of his life if she died before him. She also took a guarantee of five years. Alyson died after a year so the pension continued to pay Keith £10,000 a year for four years after which it reduced to £5,000 a year for the rest of his life.

Insight

If you take 100% spouse's pension you don't really need this guarantee but it is a popular option for those who take less than 100% as it costs very little to do so.

A pension that is paid in advance or arrears

You can usually choose to have your pension paid monthly, quarterly or yearly. The pension can be paid at the beginning of the period or at the end of it, i.e. in advance or arrears. A pension paid in arrears will pay a slightly higher amount than one paid in advance.

Insight

As most people take a pension paid monthly there is hardly any difference between the rates for a pension paid in advance compared with one paid in arrears.

A pension that will return a lump sum if you die before the age of 75

It is possible to take out a degree of capital protection if you die before the age of 75. The age of 75 is the limit set by HMRC in the rules for all pensions.

The way this protection works is that you protect a percentage up to 100% of the pension fund you use to buy the pension. If you die before all of the fund has been paid to you in the form of income, the difference will be repaid to your estate or spouse less tax of 35%.

Example

Ian Skidmore was 65 and had a pension fund of £100,000 which bought him a pension of £7,000 a year. He also elected for 100% capital protection. He died at the age of 70 so he would have received a total of £35,000 of pension income. The pension provider returned the difference of £65,000 less tax of £22,750 to his estate.

Insight

The idea of capital protect appeals to a lot of people as it reassures them that the saving they have worked so hard to build up will not be lost if they die soon after taking out the pension. However, single people usually prefer to have the higher income while they are alive. Married people tend to take a spouse's pension so when they see the figures many feel that they don't really need the capital protection.

Pension drawdown

Up until this point we have only considered buying an annuity with your pension fund. The advantage of an annuity is that it can never run out as long as you are alive and you are guaranteed a certain level of income.

However, a number of alternatives to taking an annuity are available. The most common of these is something known as drawdown, or to give it its technical name, unreserved pension.

With drawdown you don't convert your pension fund to annuity, instead you draw an income directly from the pension fund, hence its name.

Not every pension offers drawdown, in fact most do not. If you want to do this you may need to move your pension to a provider who does.

The advantages of drawdown are:

▶ *You may be able to obtain a higher income than you would buying an annuity.*
▶ *You can take the lump sum without an income.*
▶ *There is still the potential for the fund to grow and therefore for you to take an increased pension.*
▶ *If you die your fund is not lost.*

The main disadvantages are:

▶ *Your income is not guaranteed and could fall in the future.*
▶ *After age 75 the drawdown rules change.*

We will now look at these points in a little more detail.

You may be able to obtain a higher income than you would buying an annuity

You can take any level of drawdown between 0% and 120% of the Government Actuaries Department (GAD) annuity rate. On the face of it, the fact that you can take 120% implies that you will be able to secure a higher income this way than buying an annuity. Thus, if the GAD rate enabled you to take a pension of £10,000 from a pension of £100,000, then you could take £12,000 with drawdown.

However, an annuity rate set by a government department is not always the best annuity rate on the market – you can nearly always buy a higher annuity than this rate. If you are in good health you will still normally be able to obtain more initially from a drawdown than an annuity, but the figure is rarely as high as 120%. If you smoke or have any medical conditions you may find that you can secure a higher income through buying an annuity higher than you could through drawdown.

You can take the lump sum without an income
If you select an income of 0% it is fairly obvious that you will not draw any income from your pension but you can take the tax-free lump sum. Although it sounds like it is playing with words, HMRC rules state that the lump sum must be paid at the same time as the income commences, but they do allow that income to be nothing!

There is still the potential for the fund to grow and therefore for you to take an increased pension

Because you don't convert your pension fund to an annuity your pension remains invested and the fund may continue to grow meaning that you may be able to increase the amount of drawdown you can take from the fund. However the opposite is also true and the fund could fall in value.

Insight
Choosing an appropriate fund for a pension in drawdown is one of the most difficult aspects of the whole process.

Too conservative and it will not keep up with the income being taken, too adventurous and you risk it falling in value which will also mean a reduced income.

If you die your fund is not lost

With drawdown if you die before the age of 75, your relatives will have a number of choices about what happens with any of the fund that hasn't been drawn. If you are married or in civil partnership, your partner can choose to either take drawdown in his or her own right or use the fund to buy an annuity. Alternatively they can ask for the fund to be paid out as a lump sum. If they decide to take the lump sum then it will be subject to tax at 35%.

In some ways all of these options are available under an annuity as you can elect to take a spouse's pension and/or capital protection but they have to be chosen at the outset and will reduce the amount of income payable. With drawdown the amount of income is not reduced because at that stage no spouse's pension is selected and the choice about what to do on death is made at the time.

Insight

It is this flexibility of how benefits are paid on death that is one of the main attractions for drawdown.

Your income is not guaranteed and could fall in the future

The amount you can take as drawdown has to be reviewed at least every five years and ideally should be done more often than this.

At that stage the amount of income you can draw is reassessed based on the then current GAD rates applying for your age and the amount of money in the fund.

Obviously if your fund hasn't kept pace with the amount you have drawn from it, you can easily see that the income you take may have to be reduced, but there is another factor to take into account.

You would expect that annuity rates would increase as you get older because you have less time to live and this would compensate at least to some degree for any fall in the value of the fund. If all other things were equal this would be true, but annuity rates are not only based on life expectancy but also investment returns, in particular government gilt rates.

These rates continually change and if they fall significantly between reviews you could be faced with the situation that even if your fund has increased in value the amount of income could be reduced.

Insight

It is this uncertainty that is the biggest disadvantage with drawdown. If you decide to use drawdown rather than buy an annuity the possibility always exists that at some stage in the future your income will be reduced. In my experience if you are taking the full 120% your fund needs to grow at about 7–8% a year in order to avoid having to reduce your income at some stage in the future. This is achievable but not without some degree of investment risk.

After age 75 the drawdown rules change

You can stop taking drawdown at any stage and buy an annuity instead, but at age 75 you must either buy an annuity or use something known as an Alternatively Secured Pension. This works in the same basic way as a drawdown, the key difference being the amount of income has to be between 55% and 90% of the GAD figure for a 75-year-old.

What this means is that you will usually be able to secure a higher income through an annuity.

The rules relating to death benefits also change, which means in practice the only option is to take a spouse's pension, provided of course you have a spouse for the pension to be paid to.

Example – drawdown v annuity

Drawdown is generally thought to be worth considering if your pension fund is relatively large, say £100,000 or more. This is because it can be reasonably expensive for smaller amounts especially as it needs to be reviewed on a regular basis.

> To my mind what is just as important is what proportion of your overall retirement income does it represent and could you maintain an acceptable standard of living if the income you took from drawdown fell substantially.

Narrowing down your options

If like most people you decide to buy an annuity with your pension fund you will need a way to narrow down the options that are available to you, otherwise you will be swamped with all the different permutations. Even the basic choices a pension provider will send to you can be confusing enough and usually these are only some of those available.

To help you do this, turn back to the questions posed in Chapter 2 and complete the table below. In the first column enter what you would like in a perfect world. In the next column write the bare minimum. For example, if in a perfect world you would like a pension that increased by 5% a year but would accept one that didn't increase at all, place 5% in the 'perfect world' column and 0% in the 'bare minimum' column. The insights given throughout the chapter may also help you to decide.

The assumption is that you will take the maximum tax-free lump sum from your pension so this is not covered.

Item	Perfect world	Bare minimum
How much would you like your pension to increase by each year? Nil/3%/5%/RPI		
Would you be prepared to take a With Profit Pension that may increase but could also fall in value? Yes/No		

(Contd)

Item	Perfect world	Bare minimum
What percentage of your pension would you like to be paid to your husband or wife if you died before them? Nil/50%/100%		
What percentage of unpaid pension would you like returned if you died before age 75? Nil/50%/100%		
How long would you like 100% of your pension paid if you died shortly after taking it out? Not at all/5 yrs/10 yrs		
Would you be prepared to consider drawdown? Yes/No		

TEN POINTS TO REMEMBER

1 *Although most people take an annuity you don't have to.*

2 *You have the right to move your pension to a provider that offers the option you require.*

3 *An annuity will pay you an income for as long as you live and cannot run out.*

4 *A level pension will initially provide a higher income than an increasing one but will gradually be eroded by inflation.*

5 *If you are married or in a civil partnership, you must take a spouse's pension with money built up through contracting out. For the balance, you have the choice of a single pension that will die with you or a joint pension that will continue to be paid to your partner if you die before them.*

6 *You can guarantee pension payments for up to ten years.*

7 *It is possible to protect the capital used to buy a pension annuity up to the age of 75.*

8 *A With Profits Annuity may increase in value, but can also fall although never below a certain level.*

9 *As an alternative to an annuity you can draw directly from your pension fund. This may give a higher income to start with but you risk it falling later. It is more flexible with regard to death benefits.*

10 *The best way of reducing the choices you have to a manageable number is to consider what you would require in a perfect world and then the bare minimum you need to provide the income you need.*

7

Shopping around for a better pension

In this chapter you will:
- *consider whether you would be better off moving your pension*
- *learn what you need to do to shop around*
- *learn what to look for when shoppng around for a pension*

In the previous chapters we explained what choices you have when it comes to taking benefits from your pension.

Once you have narrowed down the options you will be in a position to obtain quotes for how much pension you can buy. As well as approaching your existing provider, it also pays to shop around to see if you can get a higher income elsewhere.

Insight

A large part of my business is shopping around to see if I can get a better pension for my clients. Occasionally their existing provider offers the best deal, but nine times out of ten we can do better for them. The amounts vary: 10% extra is usually the minimum and increases of 30% or more are not unusual. If they smoke or have medical conditions, the difference can be even higher.

If you have a defined benefit pension, it is unlikely that you will benefit from shopping around, except in a few limited circumstances that will be explained later. However, if you have a defined contribution pension you should always check to see if you could obtain a higher pension elsewhere. The probability of obtaining an increased pension is even higher if you smoke, are overweight or have a medical condition.

It has been estimated that only four out of the ten people who retire every year with pensions switch pension providers, even when it is beneficial to do so. If you think that you will only have one opportunity to buy your pension income, and the income you buy will last the rest of your life, then if you do nothing else covered in this book, following the advice in this chapter could repay the cover price many hundreds or even thousands of times over.

How much difference could shopping around make?

The table below shows the difference between the best and tenth best pension as listed by the FSA (at the time of writing) for a person with a pension fund of £100,000 both in good and in poor health.

	Tenth best pension	Best pension if in good health	Best pension if in poor health
Female: age 60	£5,694	£6,384	£8,560
Male: age 65	£6,816	£7,452	£10,323

Note that these are just the top ten providers shown in the FSA tables and many providers will have even lower rates than the tenth best shown here. Furthermore, the difference isn't a single increase but one that will last every year until the day you die. Also, note that rates constantly change so the differential could be more or less than this when you take your pension.

DEFINED BENEFIT PENSION SCHEMES

If you have a defined benefit pension scheme, either as a current member or one that you have left, it is unlikely you will be able to improve on the pension being offered by your employer or former employer.

However, very occasionally the opposite will be true, especially if you do not need a spouse's pension or are in ill health. If either or both of these situations apply it is worth investigating to see if you would be better off taking your pension elsewhere.

Insight

The occasions when you would be better off leaving your defined benefit pension to take a pension elsewhere will be very rare indeed. If an adviser suggests that you do this be extremely wary and expect them to point out at least as many drawbacks as benefits. Be very clear about how much money they will earn by you moving pensions.

Even if you decide to move your defined benefit pension you need to be sure you match like for like, in particular inflation protection. Most defined benefit pensions have protection against inflation that can be difficult to replicate if you transfer. This may not seem a major issue whilst inflation is running at 2½–3%, but there is always the risk that inflation could rise above these figures. If that happened, over time your standard of living could be reduced substantially. Thus if the inflation provision under your existing scheme is significantly more generous than the alternative on offer, you will probably be best advised to stick with your existing scheme.

The table below shows how damaging inflation can be to your standard of living. For example, if inflation ran at 5% a year £1,000 would only be worth £598.74 after 10 years and £358.49 after 20 years.

Inflation rate	Value of £1,000 after 10 years	Value of £1,000 after 20 years
2%	£817.07	£667.61
3%	£737.42	£543.71
5%	£598.74	£358.49
8%	£434.39	£188.69
10%	£348.68	£121.58

If you do decide to investigate moving your defined benefit pension you will need to obtain a transfer value from your existing pension provider. In this instance the transfer value is 'worked back' from the pension you are entitled to using a number of assumptions. These assumptions can vary by a wide margin and will almost certainly be different to the 'lifetime allowance value' that will be shown on your pension offer.

This is because the lifetime allowance is a figure HMRC use to assess the maximum value of pension you have built up for tax purposes rather than the true value of the pension.

Insight

If you do consider transferring your defined benefit pension, either at retirement or before, you are strongly advised to obtain specialist advice as there are a number of considerations that are not immediately obvious. In fact, the FSA insists that advisers who work in this area are specially authorized and must work from the assumption that to transfer would be inappropriate.

DEFINED CONTRIBUTION PENSIONS

If you have a defined contribution pension, such as a personal pension or occupational money purchase scheme, it is *always* worth checking to see if you would be better off taking your pension annuity with a different company to the one you have built up your pensions savings with.

Insight

Some defined contribution pensions, mainly older style personal pensions such as Retirement Annuity Contracts, have a guaranteed pension rate. Because these guarantees were given a long time ago when interest rates where much higher than they are now, they will tend to be much higher than pension rates currently available or likely to be available in the foreseeable future. Even if your pension does have a guaranteed annuity rate it is still worth shopping around as:

- *you may still be able to better the rate*
- *what is on offer from your existing provider may not match your requirements; for example, it may only offer a single life rate when you require a spouse's pension.*

The reason you may be able to obtain a higher pension is because the amount of pension a company is prepared to pay varies between companies. There are a number of reasons for this. Some companies specialize in this area where others are not particularly interested. Sometimes a company may have the equivalent of a 'special offer' where they will offer a market leading rate for a short period. However, unlike the special offer on washing powder or sugar from your local supermarket, the benefit will last the rest of your life.

You may also be able to obtain a better pension by combining a lot of different pensions that you have built up over the years. Merging them into a single scheme when you retire could mean obtaining a higher income as well as meaning you don't have income coming in from a multitude of different sources.

Finally, some companies offer what is known as enhanced and impaired life annuities. One of the major factors insurance companies take into account when setting pension rates is how long they expect an average person of a given age and sex to live.

If your lifestyle or state of health means that there is the possibility that you will die before the average age, you may be able to obtain a higher pension.

Insight

You may not be surprised to learn that if you smoke you will nearly always be able to obtain a higher pension than someone that doesn't, but you may be surprised at what else will count. Slightly raised blood pressure could get you a higher pension, as could diabetes, even if you are in perfect health otherwise.

(Contd)

If any of the following apply to you then you should always investigate if you could obtain an impaired life pension:

- ▶ *if you are taking regular medication*
- ▶ *if you smoke*
- ▶ *if you have been hospitalized in the last five years*
- ▶ *if you have been referred to a medical specialist in the last five years.*

These lifestyle or health issues can be what many would consider relatively minor. You may only be an occasional smoker or suffer from slightly increased high blood pressure and still be able to obtain a higher pension. It has been estimated that 40% of people who apply for an annuity every year would be able to obtain a higher rate on health grounds.

Give the prospective pension provider or adviser as much information as possible and ensure you are totally open and honest. The exact opposite is at play here as when you buy life assurance. If you smoke 40 a day, say so, don't say 10. If you have been prescribed certain drugs, give full details as the more information you can give, the more likely you are to receive an increased pension.

What do you need to do in order to shop around?

Nearly all pensions have to offer you the right to buy your pension from another provider. This right is known as the Open Market Option.

If you are approaching the date that you said you intended to retire when you took out the plan, you should be sent what is known as a 'wake up pack' four to six months ahead of that date. This will give a number of sample pension options and, crucially, if you intend to shop around an Open Market Option (OMO) value. This is the value of the fund that you can use to buy a pension elsewhere.

If the date you want to take benefits doesn't coincide with the date you originally set you can request a pack.

Insight

You may need to look closely at the pack to find the information you need. The FSA researched this area in 2007 and found that 40% of packs issued failed to meet the regulatory requirements.

Where do you find the best rates?

There are a number of websites that compare pension annuity rates but the first place to look is the FSA comparison tables. The easiest way to find these is to type 'FSA comparison tables' into an internet search engine. Further details of how to find these are given at the end of the book.

The advantages of using the FSA tables is that you can be sure that, as the regulator, they are truly independent. The main disadvantage is that the companies that submit the rates do so on a voluntary basis. As you would expect, this tends to mean those with the best rates do submit them but this is not always the case.

Alternatively you may decide to use an Independent Financial Adviser (IFA) who will shop around for you, and if you wish, process the transfer if it is beneficial to do so. What to expect from an IFA in this situation is covered below.

Where to seek advice

If you decide that you need professional advice, an Independent Financial Adviser will be able to help you in the following ways:

They will have access to the whole market and will usually have the systems to search out the best rate for your particular circumstances. If you try to do this yourself, you will need to know which companies offer the best pension rates for you. As mentioned above, whilst the FSA have 'best buy' tables they may not cover your particular requirements.

Comparison tables are not always 100% accurate for an individual's circumstances, particularly if you are entitled to an impaired life annuity. An IFA will ask you the specific questions needed to find the precise rate for you.

Some insurance companies are notorious for the lack of information provided or for providing information in a way that is almost impossible to understand. An IFA can obtain the relevant information and explain it to you.

There are a number of catches to be aware of. Even transferring to a safer fund can sometimes have drawbacks. An adviser will be able to point these out.

WHAT TO LOOK FOR IN AN ADVISER

Ensure your adviser has the specialist skills and experience, not only to find the best rates but also to highlight the advantages and disadvantages. The best way of doing this is to ask for examples of the reports they have prepared for others in the same situation. A report should be clear, understandable and highlight disadvantages as well as advantages.

Check that you are not being encouraged to switch purely so the adviser can earn commission. The best way of avoiding this is to approach an Independent Financial Adviser and be prepared to pay a fee for the advice.

Ensure you receive the adviser's recommendation in writing before you proceed, and check that what is said matches what you have been told verbally.

WHAT SHOULD YOUR ADVISER DO?

The first thing an adviser should do is establish what sort of pension is right for you. They will do this by asking questions about your circumstances, requirements and other pensions and savings. For example, they should establish if a spouse's pension and/or a pension that increases every year should be considered.

Insight

In other words, the adviser should help you narrow down the choices available for your pension as discussed previously.

It may be that until you see the actual amounts of pension available to you, you will not be able to be definitive on how you want to take the benefits. If this is the case don't hesitate to ask for various comparisons.

If your pension is invested in a fund that could fall in value, they may well suggest moving to a fund where the risk of this happening is greatly reduced, although depending on your existing pension's terms and conditions this is not always possible.

Insight

One of the first things I do when a customer tells me that they are considering taking their pension is to see if we can move their pension fund to one that is unlikely to fall in value. This is because protecting what they have built up already is more important than any growth that may occur in the time before they take the pension. Whether or not this is possible and the extent of the protection will depend on their existing pension. In some cases we can significantly reduce the risk of the pension falling in value, sometimes reduce it a little and sometimes we just have to leave the fund where it is.

If you are within a few months of retirement you will probably have received a 'wake up' pack from your existing provider that will give a number of ways you can take the pension. Your adviser will check if these match the way you want to take your pension.

If you haven't received this quote or the quote doesn't match the way you want to take benefits, your adviser will contact your existing provider for a quote that matches what you want.

Once the details of your existing pension are known, he or she will shop around for a better pension. Most advisers who specialize in this sort of business will have access to comparison data that will tell them the best rates on a daily basis.

They will then advise you if a better pension is available elsewhere, and how much that will be, or if you are better off staying with your existing provider. They will help you decide which option or options to take. Usually, they will give you a number of choices rather than just one figure to enable you to finalize which type of pension you would prefer.

Example

Mr and Mrs Jackson wanted figures for:

▶ *a pension that paid a pension of 50% or 100% to Mrs Jackson for the rest of her life if Mr Jackson died before her.*
▶ *a pension that does not increase each year and one that increases at 3% a year.*

Pension options for Mr and Mrs Jackson:

Pension type	Level pension 100% spouse's pension	Pension increasing 3% pa 100% spouse's pension	Level pension 50% spouse's pension	Pension increasing 3% pa 50% spouse's pension
Annual Pension	£12,098	£8,987	£10,867	£9,765

By presenting the options in this way Mr Jackson can clearly see the choices available to him and this makes it easier for him to make a final decision.

If you decide to move your pension

Depending on the type of pension you have, you may have a choice of transferring the whole fund and taking the tax-free lump sum from the new provider, or taking the tax-free lump sum with the original provider and transferring the balance that will be used for buying the income. From a financial view there is no difference, the lump sum will be the same whichever way you decide.

The process of transfer will usually take four to six weeks, but in some cases it can take longer, so if you are able to take the lump sum from the original provider(s) you will tend to get your hands on it a little sooner. Against that, if you are transferring from a number of providers it might be easier to receive a single cheque from the new provider, particularly if your existing pensions are subject to different rules where some are able to pay the lump sum and transfer the balance and others where the whole value of the pension has to be transferred to the new provider.

During this time the value of your existing pension could rise or fall and this is why wherever possible the pension should be transferred to a fund where the risk of this is minimized.

To actually make the transfer involves filling in a series of forms. These forms can be somewhat daunting but don't let that put you off. Remember that by doing so you will be getting a higher income for the rest of your life. If you are using a financial adviser then they should help you complete the forms.

TEN POINTS TO REMEMBER

1 *You don't have to take your pension with the existing provider, you can shop around for a better deal.*

2 *It is unlikely you will be able to beat the pension promised from a defined benefit pension, but if you are single or in poor health you will very occasionally be better off moving.*

3 *If you do think you may be better off moving a defined benefit pension and taking the pension elsewhere make sure you compare like for like, for example taking into account what inflation protection your existing and proposed pension offers. Seek specialist advice and ask what is in it for the adviser.*

4 *If you have a defined contribution pension you should always shop around.*

5 *Some (mainly older) defined contribution pensions have guaranteed pension annuity rates, which may offer a higher income than can be obtained by shopping around. Even so it is still worth shopping around as the guarantee may be beaten and may not match your requirements.*

6 *If you smoke or have any health issues you may be eligible for an impaired life pension that will pay a higher amount.*

7 *It has been estimated that 40% of people who apply for an annuity every year would be able to obtain a higher rate on health grounds.*

8 *The FSA publish pension annuity tables where you can check to see if you are likely to be able to obtain a higher pension elsewhere.*

9 *If you use an adviser, make sure they are experienced in this area.*

10 *It can take some time for the transfer to go through, so if you can, it is worth switching to a fund that is less likely to fall in value.*

8

Tax and National Insurance

In this chapter you will learn:
- *how the tax system benefits many retired people*
- *how Income Tax works*
- *how to take advantage of Capital Gains Tax*
- *National Insurance*
- *completing tax returns*

In October 2009, an Audit Office report found that in the UK, 1.5 million pensioners were overpaying tax on their pensions, savings and investments by an average of £171 a year.

In addition, 3.2 million paid too much tax because they did not claim all their allowances and 2.4 million lost out because they did not have interest on their savings paid gross.

Insight

Most people do not understand tax at any stage in their life, but retirement is a time when it is important to have at least a basic understanding, not least in view of the reason given above. As with so much else, the detail can be fiendishly complicated but the basics are relatively straightforward.

Question: Why would a retired couple over the age of 65 only need a gross income of £25,000 to give them the same standard of living as when they were working and earning £31,700, even if their expenditure didn't reduce by a single penny?

(Contd)

Answer: Generally speaking, retired people have to pay less tax than those who are working.

Income Tax

Income Tax is generally due on any income you receive, including income from working, interest on savings, pensions and even some state benefits. In most cases, at least some of the tax will be deducted before the income reaches you. An employer is obliged by law to deduct tax before paying you and a bank or building society must deduct basic rate tax from your interest unless you notify them on an official Inland Revenue form that you do not have to pay Income Tax.

Insight

When thinking about how much income you receive, whether that income is from working, pensions, interest or any other source, you should always look at the net income you receive after tax as this is the amount you will actually receive.
For example, on an investment of £100,000 receiving 5% interest, a basic rate taxpayer will receive £4,000 a year not £5,000, and a higher rate taxpayer will only receive £3,000 or £2,500, depending on their total income.

Income Tax is payable in bands, with a different rate of tax payable on each band. You only pay the rate of tax applicable to the band. *You do not pay the highest rate on all your income.*

Until 2010 everyone had a Personal Allowance no matter how much their income was, but from April 2010 anyone earning over £100,000 has their allowance reduced by £1 for each £2 of income over the £100,000 limit until they have no allowance whatsoever.

What this means is that if an individual's income was below the Personal Allowance figure, they wouldn't pay Income Tax at all.

If it fell into the basic rate tax band then some income wouldn't be taxed at all and some would be taxed at basic rate. If it fell into the higher rate some would not be taxed at all, some would be taxed at the basic rate and some at the higher rate.

These are demonstrated in the examples below. Although these examples are based on 2010/11 tax bands and rates, the principle remains the same.

Example 1 – no Income Tax payable

Margery Roberts has an income of £4,000 a year. This falls within her Personal Allowance so she will not have to pay any Income Tax at all.

Example 2 – basic rate tax payable

Ian Walters has an income of £15,000. As he is age 63, his Personal Allowance is £6,475 so he will pay tax as follows:

Band	Rate payable	Tax payable
£6,475	Personal Allowance 0%	£0.00
£6,475–£15,000	basic rate 20%	£1,705.05
Total		£1,705.05

Example 3 – higher rate tax payable

Miriam Alexander has an income of £70,000 a year. As she is 60 her Personal Allowance is £6,475 so she will pay tax as follows:

Band	Rate payable	Tax payable
£6,475	Personal Allowance 0%	£0.00
£6,475–£37,400	basic rate 20%	£7,480.00
£37,401–£70,000	higher rate 40%	£10,450.00
Total		£17,930.00

In the example above, Miriam had to pay higher rate tax on her income over £43,895. If you had looked at the HMRC tax tables they would have stated that she would have had to pay higher rate tax on income over £37,400. This is because the higher rate starts on *taxable* income over this amount. The first £6,475 covered by her Personal Allowance does not count as taxable income, therefore higher rate tax starts at £43,895, i.e. £6,475 + £37,400.

From April 2010 the top rate of tax on income over £150,000 a year will be 50%. In addition, the Personal Allowance will be reduced for anyone with an income over £100,000 a year. As this will only apply to a small number of people, I have not included an example.

Insight

Some people worry that if their income increases over a certain limit their overall income will reduce because they will have to pay more tax. Whilst an increased income will usually result in more tax being paid, the way the UK Income Tax system works means that you can *never* have a reduced income because you fall into another Income Tax bracket.

PERSONAL ALLOWANCE

Nearly everyone is entitled to have a certain level of income before they have to pay tax (but see also the point above about incomes over £100,000). This is known as a Personal Allowance and it is available to everyone irrespective of their age, including children.

People over the age of 65 are entitled to an extra Personal Allowance known as an Age Allowance. The age of 65 applies to both men and women whether they are working or not.

This means a man or woman over the age of 65 can have an income of £9,490 (2009/10) before they have to pay any Income Tax. This allowance is increased again at age 75 to £9,640.

If your income is over a certain level, the Age Allowance is reduced by £1 for every £2 of income above the threshold level as shown in the example below. Once again the figures are based on the 2010/11 tax year.

Example 1 – full Age Allowance available

Ian Harris is 66 and has an income of £19,000 a year. The first £9,490 is not subject to tax which means he will have to pay basic rate tax on £9,510 giving him a tax bill of £1,902.

Example 2 – some Age Allowance available

Elizabeth Stone is 67 and has an income of £25,000 a year. This is above the earnings limit of £22,900 to obtain the full Age Allowance, which means it will be reduced by £1 for every £2 of income above the limit.

This means her allowance will be reduced by £1,050:

Income	£25,000
Age Allowance limit	£22,900
excess over limit	£2,100
reduction in Age Allowance	£1,050
Age Allowance therefore	£8,590

Therefore the first £8,590 will not be subject to tax, meaning she will have to pay 20% tax on £16,410 giving her a tax bill of £3,280.

Example 3 – no Personal Allowance available

Phil Michaels is 70 and has an income of £40,000 a year. This is above the earnings limit of £22,900 by £17,100. His Age Allowance will therefore be reduced by £2 for every £1 above the limit, which would give a figure of £8,550. However, the maximum Age Allowance reduction can only take a person down to the basic Personal Allowance level of £6,475, so in practice Phil's Age Allowance will be reduced by £3,010.

Insight

If you are married or in a permanent relationship it makes a great deal of sense to use the Personal and Age Allowances to your advantage by ensuring that both of you use your maximum allowances. This is explained in more detail below.

If we take an example of a couple both over the age of 65 with an income of £25,000 and all of that income is in one name, their income after tax would be £21,486. If however that gross income was split so they had an income of £12,500 each, their joint net income would be £23,612, over £2,000 more.

It is not always possible to split income in this way. For instance, you cannot split your wages or pension income, but there is often scope to split savings or investments in such a way to take advantage of your Personal Allowances.

Example 1 – Bill and Sally Richardson

Bill is 65, has recently retired and has the following annual income:

Pension	£17,000
Interest on savings	£5,000
Total	£22,000
Bill's net income after tax	£19,386

His wife Sally is 63 and has an income of:

Pension	£3,000
Sally doesn't pay tax so her net income is	£3,000
Total joint income after tax	£22,386

If they transfer the savings to Sally's name then things will look like this:

Bill's income

Pension	£17,000
Bill's net income after tax	£15,406

Sally's income

Pension	£3,000
Interest on savings	£5,000
Total	£8,000
Sally's net income after tax	£7,487
Total joint income after tax	£22,893

This gives them an extra £507 a year. In a few years time when Sally is 65, due to the Age Allowance she will not have to pay any Income Tax, giving them an extra £1,020 a year.

WHAT COUNTS AS INCOME?

Income that may be subject to Income Tax includes:

▶ *income from employment*
▶ *income from self-employment/partnerships*
▶ *pension income*
▶ *interest on savings*
▶ *investment income*
▶ *rental income*
▶ *certain state benefits.*

Income that is not subject to Income Tax includes:

▶ *interest on savings from all ISAs and PEPs*
▶ *National Savings Certificates*

- *a certain amount of rent paid by a lodger in your home*
- *tax credits*
- *some state benefits.*
- *Premium Bond winnings.*

Most income is added together and subject to basic or higher rate tax as appropriate but some income from dividends is subject to a different (lower) rate of tax.

HOW IS INCOME TAX PAID?

In most cases Income Tax is deducted at source. This means that the person paying the income is responsible for deducting the tax and paying it to HMRC.

For most forms of savings and investment, basic rate is deducted and if you are a higher rate taxpayer you will have to pay the additional amount.

If you are a non-taxpayer, whether you will be able to reclaim any tax that has been deducted will depend on the type of savings or investment. Details of the specific tax treatment for many popular types of savings are explained in Chapter 10.

Insight

If you don't pay Income Tax it is always worth asking the provider of your savings or investment plan what the position is with regard to tax and whether you can reclaim any tax that has been paid. Often if you are a non-taxpayer you can ask your provider to pay you the income without any tax deduction, but you may not be able to reclaim tax already paid.

Capital Gains Tax

Insight

In my opinion, this is probably the least understood tax in the UK. Yet if I can schedule my client's investments so they come under the Capital Gains Tax rules rather than Income Tax rules, I nearly always will. Why? Because in most cases it means they will pay less tax.

WHAT IS CAPITAL GAINS TAX?

Capital Gains Tax (CGT) is payable on any gain (i.e. increase in value) of an investment. For example, if you buy an investment for £50,000 and sell it for £59,000 you have made a profit of £9,000. This profit is subject to Capital Gains Tax.

In addition to their Income Tax allowance every year, all individuals have a Capital Gains Tax allowance. If your total gains in any given tax year are less than the allowance, then no CGT is payable.

The advantage of making the most your annual CGT allowance, along with other tax saving strategies such as ISAs, is that more of your money stays in your pocket rather than the taxman's.

WHAT IS A GAIN?

A gain occurs whenever 'you dispose of an asset'. In most cases this will mean when you sell it, but it also covers giving an asset away, or even receiving compensation for an asset that has been destroyed. An insurance payout on a building that was destroyed by fire could count as a disposal.

Certain assets are exempt from Capital Gains Tax including:

▶ *your car*
▶ *personal possessions worth up to £6,000 each, such as jewellery, paintings or antiques*
▶ *stocks and shares you hold in tax-free investment savings accounts, such as ISAs and PEPs*
▶ *UK government or 'gilt-edged' securities, e.g. National Savings Certificates, Premium Bonds and loan stock issued by the Treasury*
▶ *betting, lottery or pools winnings*

- *personal injury compensation*
- *any foreign currency held for your own or your family's personal use outside the UK (e.g. if you've made a gain because of a change to the exchange rate).*

One item you may expect to see on this list but is missing is your home. In practice you will not have to pay Capital Gains Tax on your family home, providing it is your only home and you have actually lived there. However, you will usually have to pay Capital Gains Tax on any profit you make on the disposal of any other properties you own, including buy-to-let investments and holiday homes.

Insight

In most cases a gain is the profit that occurs when an investment is sold. For example, if you have a buy-to-let property, then the rent you receive is income and if you sell the property any profit you make on its sale is a gain. In a similar way dividends from shares are treated as income whereas any profit on sale is a gain. Interest you receive on your deposit account is always income even if you don't withdraw the interest and allow it to build up.

WHAT IS THE ADVANTAGE OF CAPITAL GAINS TAX?

For most people there are two main advantages of having an investment subject to Capital Gains Tax rather than Income Tax and these are:

- *most people don't use their Capital Gains Tax allowance but do use their Income Tax allowance*
- *the rate for Capital Gains Tax is less than Income Tax.*

Both of these points are illustrated in the example below:

Example

Bob Richards is 65 and about to retire. He will receive £5,200 state pension and a company pension of £25,000 a year. He also has £90,000 savings and will receive £75,000 tax-free cash from his pension.

He can comfortably live on his income and would like to invest his £165,000 capital for some stage in the future. He would like to consider saving this money for at least five years. For simplicity in this example, we will ignore the possibility of Bob using an ISA, although in practice this should always be considered.

If Bob received 5% a year interest on his £165,000, because he would have to pay Income Tax on this interest after tax he would have made £35,747.75. If however he had arranged his investment so instead of interest it made a capital gain of 5% a year and was therefore subject to Capital Gains Tax, then he would have made £39,108.89, an additional £3,361.14.

With some additional relatively simple tax planning, Bob may have been able to avoid paying any Capital Gains Tax at all, meaning his return would have been £45,586.46, nearly £10,000 more than an investment subject to Income Tax.

CAPITAL GAINS TAX ALLOWANCE AND TAX RATE

Every year you have a Capital Gains Tax allowance. In the tax year 2009/10 this amount was £10,100 although it tends to go up every year. The allowance applies to all of your disposals in the tax year, and it can't usually be carried forward to another tax year.

Example

In tax year 2009/10, Mary King sold a buy-to-let property and made a profit of £50,000. In the same tax year she also sold shares on which her profit was £10,000, making her total gain in that year £60,000. The first £10,100 was not subject to tax, leaving her to pay tax on £49,900. In this tax year the Capital Gains Tax rate was 18% meaning she would have to pay tax of £8,982.

HOW IS CAPITAL GAINS TAX ACTUALLY PAID?

Unlike Income Tax which is often deducted before you receive your income, you are personally responsible for calculating any

Capital Gains Tax that is due. You have to declare this on your tax return and the tax is actually payable on 31 January in the tax year following the disposal.

> ## Insight
>
> There is an old saying that you shouldn't let the tax tail wag the investment dog. What this means is the tax treatment of an investment should be the last thing you should consider, and not the first. This is very true and the most important aspect when choosing savings or an investment is making sure it is right for your individual circumstances in particular your views on investment risk.

National Insurance

When National Insurance (NI) was originally introduced the amount raised was supposed to more or less match the things it paid for, such as the NHS and state pensions. Over the years this has changed and now it is just another form of personal taxation, although payment of NI contributions are needed to earn entitlement to certain state benefits, including the basic state pension.

It is sometimes called a tax on employment as it is only payable on income received from being employed or self-employed.

> ## Insight
>
> The key points about National Insurance when considering retirement are:
>
> ▶ *It is not payable on pension or savings income.*
> ▶ *It is not payable by anyone over state retirement age on any income.*

It is not payable on pension or savings income
The relevance of NI not being paid on pension or savings income is important in taking into account how much income you will

actually 'take home' in retirement. If you earned £15,000 a year from employment, you would take home after tax and NI £1,022.80 a month (2009/10 tax year). That same £15,000 from a pension would give you an income of £1,107.92, an extra £85 a month.

It is not payable by anyone over state retirement age on any income
If you are over state retirement age, then you do not have to pay NI on any income even if you are working.

So that NI is not deducted you will need to provide your employer with an Age Exemption Certificate. This should be sent to you when you reach state retirement age but if you do not receive one then you can obtain one by writing to or phoning HM Revenue and Customs. The contact details are at the end of the book.

Completing tax returns

When you retire, it is highly likely you will be asked to complete a tax return on a regular basis, even if you have never had to complete one before. The main reason for this is that you are probably receiving income from a number of different sources all with a different tax office. For example, you may have income from the state pension, a company pension and a personal pension as well as any savings and investments. These all need to be taken into account to assess how much tax you should pay.

As indicated at the beginning of this chapter it is probably more likely that in retirement you will pay more tax than you should rather than less, so accurately completing a tax return can go a long way to avoid this.

Insight

Whilst a tax return may look daunting, these days they are not as difficult to complete as you may first think. The sheer number of pages are there to cover a wide range of

(Contd)

eventualities and you will probably find that most do not apply to you. The secret of being able to complete your tax return without too much pain is to keep accurate records of your financial transactions.

For example, if you have a deposit account the provider should send you a statement every year showing how much interest has been paid and tax deducted; the same is true for investments. Apart from making it easier for you to complete a tax return, if you decide you need help with it, then having all the documentation will help the person doing this for you to be as accurate as possible and avoid you paying too much tax.

It is also probable that when you first retire that you will be sent a form by HMRC asking you to write down all your sources of income. The reason for this is the same as the reason you may receive a tax return, i.e. your income is likely to come from a number of different sources all with different tax offices. Unless they are told otherwise, the organization paying you your income will usually do so without applying your Personal Allowance which could result in you paying more tax than you need to.

TEN POINTS TO REMEMBER

1 *Income tax is payable in bands.*

2 *Everyone except those with a very high income are entitled to a Personal Allowance.*

3 *You do not pay Income Tax on any income up to the Personal Allowance level.*

4 *At the age of 65 you are allowed a higher Personal Allowance, known as the Age Allowance, before you pay tax.*

5 *If your income is over a certain level the Age Allowance is gradually reduced but never below the level of the Personal Allowance, unless you have an income over £100,000 in which case your Personal Allowance will be reduced irrespective of your age.*

6 *For a couple it makes a great deal of sense (if you can) to split your income to make the most of the Personal Allowance and Age Allowance.*

7 *If you don't pay Income Tax ask your savings or investment provider if you can be paid your interest or other income without deduction of tax.*

8 *Capital Gains Tax is payable on the disposal of an asset. This will usually mean when it is sold, but other factors can also count.*

9 *You have a Capital Gains Tax allowance which means the first part of your gains are not subject to tax.*

10 *The rate for Capital Gains Tax is lower than for Income Tax, so it is worth considering saving in investments subject to Capital Gains Tax as you will usually pay less tax.*

9

Investment basics

In this chapter you will learn:
- *about investment wrappers*
- *about assessing the risk of an investment and your attitude to that risk*
- *about the four asset classes: cash, fixed interest, property and equities*
- *about different types of funds*

When a person is working they can build up capital by saving from their income. Their ability to do this may stop, or at least be greatly reduced, upon retirement. Furthermore the capital accumulated to this point will often have to last the rest of their lives.

This may create a dilemma, particularly if you have to rely on income generated by that capital in order to maintain your standard of living. Putting the money in the building society will be safe but may not create the growth or income you need or want, especially at times when interest rates are low. On the other hand, you may not be in a position to recover any money lost on more adventurous investments.

This chapter will point out the basic 'mechanics' of investing including:

▶ *the difference between the investment itself and the investment wrapper*
▶ *what is wanted from the investment*
▶ *understanding investment risk*

► *understanding different asset classes*
► *understanding managed investments.*

Insight

One of the most common errors when it comes to understanding savings and investments is to confuse the investment 'wrapper' or 'vehicle' with the investment itself. You may reject the idea of a Unit Trust for fear of it being too risky, however a Unit Trust only really refers to the tax treatment structure of an investment rather than where your money is actually invested. In fact a wide range of Unit Trust investments are available from the very cautious to the highly adventurous.

Wrappers, vehicles and investments

A 'wrapper' is the jargon used to describe the mechanics and more particularly the tax treatment of an investment. A 'vehicle' is another term used for exactly the same thing. All the following are types of investment wrappers:

► *ISAs*
► *bonds*
► *Unit Trusts*
► *Open-Ended Investment Companies (OEICs)*
► *pensions.*

The investment itself is where the money is actually placed. For example, in fixed interest accounts or shares. In this day and age it is possible to access the same type of investment through any of these wrappers and often it is possible to access exactly the same investment through all of them.

Insight

When it comes to investment most people approach the issue from the wrong 'end', starting with the investment wrapper and often going no further. The best approach is to start with what is required from the investment, then decide on the investment itself and the investment wrapper.

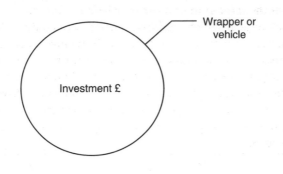

What do you want from your savings or investment?

Savings or investments can only achieve one or both of two objectives. They can produce an income, or growth, or a mixture of both. In practice as well as grow they can also fall in value, but we will return to this later.

The term 'savings' tends to be used to describe putting money away on a regular basis in low-risk areas, such as deposit accounts, and the term 'investing' is used when lump sums are placed in higher-risk areas. In practice there is considerable overlap between the two. The key point is not to worry about the label but to think about what you want for your money.

Questions to ask before even considering where to save or invest
Before even considering where you should place your money ask yourself the following questions:

▶ *How much do you currently have saved or invested?*
▶ *Is that amount likely to increase at some time in the future?*

- ▸ *If so, by how much?*
- ▸ *Do you have to use your savings to generate an income?*
- ▸ *Do you want to use your savings to increase your income?*
- ▸ *If yes, how much income do you need or want?*
- ▸ *Is that need likely to increase or decrease in the future?*
- ▸ *If yes, by how much and when?*

If you need or want income, in an ideal world you will want to generate all the income you need without taking any risk at all. In practice this may not be possible, so if you had to compromise which of the following are you most likely to do?

- ▸ *reduce the amount of income you take?*
- ▸ *erode your capital?*
- ▸ *take a greater risk?*

If you don't need income from your savings now, will you need it at some stage in the future?

Once again, in an ideal world you would want to achieve both the income you require and capital growth, but if you had to choose one over the other, which would be most important? Income or capital growth?

If you are saving or investing for capital growth, do you foresee a specific need for that capital at some time in the future, for example to buy a car or use for holidays?

At this stage you may not be able to be precise about the answers to these questions, but giving some thought to them will help you more precisely focus on the right savings or investment for you. It will also help if you decide to seek professional help as once again it will help your adviser tailor his or her recommendations to your requirements.

Only when you have answered these questions will you be in a position to decide where to save or invest.

Understanding investment risk

Insight

Whole books have been written on the subject of investment risk and hundreds of academic studies have investigated the subject, and yet no one can really predict how an investment will perform in all circumstances. Events in 2008 and 2009 have reminded us that even the safest investments can sometime be at risk. After more than 30 years working in financial services I am more convinced than ever that there are only two truths. Firstly, don't put all your eggs in one basket. Secondly, the time you intend to save or invest for is an essential consideration in deciding where to invest.

Risk is all around us every day. We can't abolish it, we can only attempt to deal with it, but whatever we do we must accept that it exists. For example, every time we go out of the house there is a risk that we could be run over, if it there is a storm, we could be struck by lightning, or if it is sunny we are at risk of skin cancer. One way of dealing with this would be to sit indoors all day, but if we did that life would be pretty boring and even then there is a risk the house could catch fire! These may all seem rather far-fetched and ridiculous extremes, but they could happen and yet we live our lives on a day-to-day basis.

In the same way, no matter what anyone, particularly someone who is trying to sell you something, tells you, there is no such thing as a risk-free savings plan or investment. It doesn't exist, it has never existed and it probably never will. Sure some savings and investments have an extremely low risk, but a risk still exists.

To understand this a little better we need to understand two risk concepts, frequency and severity. In the UK the risk of rain is very high, it has a high frequency, but the damage done to the country as a whole by floods is not that severe when compared to some other parts of the world. (Please accept my apologies if you have suffered from a flood or live in an area subject to flooding. I know it is extremely distressing and I am not dismissing it, but I am talking about the country as a whole.)

On the other hand, the chances of the country being hit by an earthquake registering 10 on the Richter Scale is very low in terms of frequency and if it did happen the consequences would be extremely severe.

We can apply the same principle to savings and investments. Until recently it was beyond most of our wildest dreams that a bank or building society could fail, and yet in 2008 some in the UK would have done if it hadn't been for government intervention.

Sometimes the news coverage tended to focus on the negative aspects of this intervention, but if one or more of our major banks had failed the impact could have been devastating, not just for the bankers, but also for the millions of ordinary people with savings.

Such an event may be considered rare, or to put it another way have a low frequency, but the consequences would have been severe.

Insight

Understanding this concept is important in realizing that there is no such thing as a risk-free investment. Who would have thought that until a few years ago many of our well-known banks would need to be bailed out by the government? The frequency of a major bank failing is low, but the severity high.

RISK AND REWARD

The general view is that the more risk you take with an investment, the greater the potential return or reward. To some degree this is true, but as with anything to do with money, things are slightly more complex than this. As always there will be times when exceptions occur, for example it is, or at least until 2009 was, generally accepted that if you invested in the stock market for ten years or more then you would almost certainly make a profit. But for the period 1999–2009, if you had invested in the FTSE 100 you would have made a loss.

This may be highly unusual and is as much to do with the market being overpriced ten years ago as it is to do with the falls in 2008/9, and may not be repeated again this century, but no one can say this for sure.

Insight

The example above also highlights the importance of not being too drawn in by sweeping generalizations. I stated the often used term 'invested in the stock market' and then used the FTSE 100 as the example. The FTSE 100 consists of the 100 biggest companies in the UK by share price. It is not by any means the only way you can invest in the stock market. For example, over the same period (until October 1999–October 2009) the best performing Unit Trust fund investing mainly in FTSE company shares, but being selective about the shares it picked, returned an average of 6.67% a year.

The truth of the matter is that a cautious investment such as a deposit account is likely to produce a steady but modest return. At the other end of the scale a more adventurous investment such as the stock market *may* produce a higher return, but may result in a loss and will rise and fall along the way.

THE DESTINATION AND THE JOURNEY

As well as frequency and severity, the aspects of risk that are more likely to impact on us on a day-to-day basis are:

▶ *risk to capital*
▶ *volatility*

Risk to capital is fairly straightforward. It means that there is the chance that you will lose all or some of the money at the end of the investment term.

Volatility is the amount that an investment will rise and fall during the time you hold it. Volatility is the most common measure of risk used by investment managers.

Insight

I refer to these concepts as the 'destination' and the 'journey'. Think of it this way. Imagine you wanted to go to Australia for a holiday. If the only way of getting there involved a three-month overland trip in the back of a truck on unmade roads and through several war zones, for most of us it will lose some appeal. However, if the option involves flying there in first class comfort then it will probably have a greater appeal. The same applies to investments. Whilst the idea of a higher return at the end may be attractive, we also need to consider how we will sleep if the investment falls a great deal during the journey.

Imagine the situation where you have invested a lump sum for five years and a year later it has fallen by 20%, but by the end of the five years it has made a total return of 30%. If you had withdrawn that investment at the end of the first year you would have actually lost 20%.

In other words, as well as considering the potential for reward you also need to consider how much volatility you could take and still sleep at night.

Insight

As a financial adviser I am often asked why I can't tell my clients to move out of an investment just before it falls and move into one just before it rises. The answer is that without a crystal ball I can't tell when these events will happen! Sometimes you can tell that something is overpriced and that it will probably fall at some stage in the future. In the same way sometimes things are obviously underpriced, but knowing precisely when and by how much is impossible.

LIVING WITH RISK

It may seem that unless you put your money in a bank you are doomed to sleepless nights and losing all of your money. This isn't true and you can take several simple steps that will go a long way to achieving what is right for you.

▶ *Start by adding up all of your savings and investments.*
▶ *Then work out how much money you would need to access quickly.*
▶ *Give some thought over how long you are prepared to invest for.*
▶ *Think about how much you could lose without it affecting your standard of living.*
▶ *Finally, ask yourself how much you would be prepared to see the value fall before you couldn't sleep at night.*

Add up all your capital
By adding up all of your existing savings and investments you can get a clearer picture of how you may then want to save or invest. For example, if you have £100,000 you may decide that you want to keep £90,000 in a secure deposit account and be extremely adventurous with the other £10,000. Alternatively you may feel more comfortable with putting £50,000 in a deposit account and £50,000 in a slightly more adventurous investment.

Work out how much you would need to access quickly
Everyone should have an emergency fund that they can access quickly if they need to. Views differ on how much this should be, but an amount equal to three months' income is often quoted.

This money should only ever be invested in safe, easily accessible investments such as deposit accounts.

Give some thought to how long you are prepared to invest for
If you can or only want to invest for a short period of time then only a deposit account or similar low-risk investment is likely to be suitable for most people. Over a longer period, say five years or more, you may want to move up the risk scale as you will

usually have time to ride out the ups and downs of an investment rising and falling.

Think about how much you could afford to lose without it affecting your standard of living
By asking yourself this question you will be better able to decide where to invest. You may decide that you could afford to lose 10% of your capital without it materially affecting your lifestyle, in which case you may be prepared to invest that 10% in a high-risk area. Alternatively any reduction in capital could have a major impact on you so you might only be prepared to invest in cautious investments.

Consider how much you would be prepared to see your investment fall and still sleep at night
With the exception of deposit style investments, most investments will fall from time to time. You need to consider how much you could tolerate before you would lose sleep. In part this is linked to the amount you invest. If you have only invested a small amount in high-risk areas you may be prepared to stand big falls in value, but the opposite is likely to be true if you invest a large amount of your capital in cautious investments.

Asset classes

Insight

I would expect the majority of people who read this book to choose some form of savings or investment where their money is managed for them on a day-to-day basis. This type of investment is discussed later in this chapter. Nonetheless, having a basic understanding of where your money will be invested can help you understand the risks involved.

Whilst there are thousands of variations on a theme, nearly every type of saving or investment falls into one or more asset classes. This is the term used to describe the characteristics of that investment. It will come as no surprise to find out that there is no single agreement on how many asset classes there actually are, but most do agree that there are four main ones, namely:

▶ *cash*
▶ *fixed interest*
▶ *commercial property*
▶ *equities.*

It is also possible to invest in areas which do not fit neatly into one of these asset classes. Gold comes quickly to mind, and these days it is also relatively easy to invest other areas such as timber or agriculture.

Over the longer term, investments within an asset class will tend to display similar characteristics to other investments in some class.

When you are saving or investing, you usually want to invest in a number of different areas to avoid putting all of your eggs in one basket.

The characteristics of the main asset classes are explained below.

CASH

When we use the expression 'cash', we are using it in a wider sense than just the notes and coins in our purse or wallet. For example, a deposit account would fall into this category, as would Premium Bonds and less well known investments such as Treasury Bonds and Commercial Bills.

Investing in cash works by you letting someone else, such as a bank, have use of your money and in return they pay interest on the amount for either an unspecified period, for example in an instant access account, or for a specified period, such as a two-year fixed rate bond.

....

Insight

The word 'bond' is the most over-used word in the whole of financial services. It is used to describe a wide variety of

(Contd)

different things, so whenever you see the word 'bond' used
to describe a savings plan or investment, look more closely to
see what you are actually buying.

Cash will have the following characteristics:

- *There will usually be a high degree of capital preservation.
  Unless the institution holding your money fails, you will
  usually get back at least what you have put in.*
- *There will be limited opportunity for rates of return above
  inflation. One of the main problems with cash is that the rates
  of return are usually less than inflation. So whilst in one sense
  your capital is preserved, what you can buy with it over the
  years will gradually reduce.*
- *It is usually highly liquid. This means unless you have signed
  up for a fixed term you can get your hands on your money
  quickly and easily.*
- *It usually pays interest which is taxed as income. We will
  explore the taxation treatment of specific investments in the
  chapters that follow.*

FIXED INTEREST

Fixed interest is similar to cash in the sense that money is lent to
a government, institution or company and they pay interest on
that money. At the end of a given period (although sometimes the
period is open ended) the capital is repaid.

The difference from cash is that, usually, the rate of interest is fixed
and you can buy or sell the investment at any time, provided of
course someone else is prepared to sell or buy. Also, unlike cash, as
well as interest received, it is possible to make a capital gain or loss
on your investment.

Perhaps the most well known example of this type of asset are
Government Bonds (that word again!) more commonly known as
gilts. The amount of interest that you receive depends as much on
how much you pay for them as the actual rate of interest. Whether

you make a gain or a loss will depend on the price you can sell them for as shown in the example below.

Example

Bill Gilles buys 100 gilts for £20,000, i.e. £200 each. The face value of each gilt is £100 and pays an interest rate of 8% based on the face value. Because Bill paid £200 for each one, the effective interest rate is 4% not 8%. The gilts are due to be repaid in ten years time and two years after buying them Bill decides to sell because the market price has risen to £250 for each gilt. This makes Bill a profit of £5,000. However, if Bill could only sell them for £150 each he would have made a loss of £5,000, and if he had held on to the them until they were redeemed he would make a loss of £10,000 as he would only receive £100 for each one.

You may ask why anyone would want to buy £100-gilts for £250, or even why Bill would want to buy them for £200. The answer is in the interest rate. If Bill could only obtain 2% interest rate from a deposit account, then 4% looks very attractive. If the deposit rate fell even further, then 4% would look even better which is why investors would be willing to pay a higher amount. If on the other hand the deposit rate rose to 3%, then 4% is starting to look less attractive and hence the price will fall.

As you may expect, in practice the price is governed by a number of factors as well as comparative interest rates, for example how much people think interest rates will rise or fall in the future has a bearing as well as how long the gilt has to run before it ends.

Fixed interest will have the following characteristics:

▶ *Fixed interest investments vary in terms of capital preservation from very high to very low and everything in between. As well as the relationship between the price paid and the price sold, the financial strength of the organization issuing them is relevant. For example, a government gilt is considered to be one of the securest investments you can buy. On the other hand, a small company will potentially pose a higher risk than a big commercial company like BP.*

▶ *Provided the organization issuing them is still in business you are guaranteed to obtain the face value at redemption.*

▶ *Historically, fixed interest investments have provided a reasonable protection against inflation, but in practice much will depend on the price you pay and the price you sell.*

▶ *Most fixed interest investments, particularly from governments and large organizations are reasonably liquid (in other words easy to buy and sell quickly) but the price varies according to supply and demand.*

▶ *Interest is usually subject to Income Tax*

PROPERTY

Property includes not just residential property such as buy-to-lets, but also commercial property such as offices, warehouses, shops and offices. In fact, if you invest in property through some form of fund rather than buying it directly, it will almost certainly only cover commercial property.

Insight

We all feel we understand property and that as an investment we can't possibly go wrong. Certainly historically over time property has proven to be a very good investment, and generally speaking its value has risen above inflation and been less volatile than the stock market. Nonetheless, if we are investing in property either directly through a buy-to-let or through some form of investment we need to be aware of the cons as well as the pros.

When investing in property specifically as an investment (as opposed to hoping to benefit from any increase in the value from our own home) we do so in the expectation that we make money from the rents received and through the capital appreciation on the property.

Property will have the following characteristics:

▶ *Historically property tends to produce steady, long-term returns above inflation, but as we saw recently this is not* always the case. Like all other investments, property can be subject to a 'bubble'.

▶ It is the most illiquid of all the four main asset classes. Even when the market is buoyant, it can be time-consuming and expensive to buy or sell a property.

▶ Over the longer term, property tends to produce returns above fixed interest and below equity.

▶ Usually low correlation with other asset classes. What this means is that property will not tend to move up or down in price in line with other assets but it will rise and fall at different times. However, once again events at the end of the last decade have proven that this is not always the case.

EQUITIES

The last asset class to be discussed here are equities or, as they are more commonly known, stocks and shares, although technically speaking in the UK stocks are fixed interest investments.

A share is so called because it represents part ownership (or a share) in the company that has issued them. We can make money from them in one of two main ways. Firstly, we have the right to share in that company's profits through any dividend the company pays and, secondly, hopefully over time those shares will rise in value and, if we sell them, we can make a capital gain.

There are two main ways most people buy shares. Either they buy them directly in the company or through some form of investment such as a pension or Unit Trust. Whichever way we do this we must understand that as part-owners of the company we will feature last in any share-out if the company fails, which is one of the reasons shares are considered to be more risky than the other asset classes.

Equities will have the following characteristics:

▶ Equities pose the highest risk to capital out of all the investment classes. If the company fails we could lose everything we have invested.

- *They tend to experience the greatest fluctuations in value of all asset classes, are rarely steady in price, constantly rising and falling in value, sometimes by a great deal.*
- *Whilst the years 1999–2009 would appear to disprove this, shares have the greatest potential for above inflation returns, especially over the longer term.*
- *They also have the greatest potential for loss, especially in the short term*
- *Liquidity varies. Shares in companies quoted on a stock market can usually be bought and sold almost instantly. Shares in a company that is not quoted on the stock market will be much harder to buy and sell as you will need to find someone who is prepared to sell or buy.*

OTHER ASSET TYPES

There is a wide range of other investments that do not fit into the asset classes shown above. The range and diversity is too great to explain here, or indeed in any single book.

Alternative assets such as these are increasingly being used by professional fund managers to achieve diversity in their funds, which in turn can reduce the investment risk of the fund.

BRINGING IT ALL TOGETHER

The most important point to make at this stage is that it is highly unlikely that any one asset type on its own will be right for you. If you want to be as certain as possible that the capital value of your savings will not fall in the short term, then cash is really the only answer.

Apart from this exception, in order to see your savings grow and or generate an income over and above inflation, you will need to invest in one or more of the other asset classes as well as cash. The skill is getting the right blend for your own personal circumstances.

To do this most people will use some form of managed fund either bought directly or through a financial adviser.

Managed savings and investments

Whilst some people will arrange every aspect of their own investment, for example they will decide on the balance that is right for them and then choose which specific investments to buy, the vast majority will save or invest through some form of fund.

The next chapters will discuss in detail the various different types of savings and investments that are available, but in the main this covers the wrapper rather than the investment itself so this section explains the main characteristics of a managed investment irrespective of the wrapper.

Before going any further it is worth explaining what is meant by the term 'fund'. A fund refers to where your money is invested. Funds can be specific, only investing in one type of asset, for example oil or government gilts, or managed funds where they will invest in a number of different types of asset, for example a mix of cash, fixed interest and equities.

There is a vast range of funds available. At the time of writing, one fund research tool listed 17,886 different funds. Most of these are specialist funds but the same source lists 1,314 balanced managed funds alone.

WHAT TYPE OF FUNDS EXIST?

We can break down the types of funds that exist in a number of different ways but for our purposes we will consider just two:

▶ *asset specific v managed funds*
▶ *passive funds v active funds*

Asset specific funds
Asset specific funds invest in a specific type of asset, in a specific part of the world. For example, there are funds that invest

in UK gilts and others that invest in Japanese Smaller Companies.

The disadvantage of investing in these types of funds as an individual investor is that not only do you have to pick the right funds, but in order to have the right balance of investments for your individual circumstances, you have to pick the right mix as well. Which means many people will select some form of managed fund.

Managed funds

The main categories of managed funds are:

- *defensive managed*
- *cautious managed*
- *balanced managed*
- *adventurous managed.*

These descriptions reflect the make-up of the fund. A balanced managed fund will invest more in equities than a cautious fund, and an adventurous fund more still. In theory this makes selecting a fund simple. If you are cautious you would simply select the best performing cautious fund.

However, this hides a wide range. For example, one definition of a cautious managed fund states that between 20% and 60% will be invested in equities. By this you can easily see that a fund investing in 20% equities will tend to be less volatile than one with 60% invested in this area. Furthermore this range allows the fund manager to adjust the equity content between these limits so there is no guarantee that if you select a fund with a low equity content it will continue that way.

On top of this there is a wide difference between the best and worst performing funds. At the time of writing, the best performing cautious managed Unit Trust/OIEC had returned 59.6% over five years against an average of 19.9% and the worst fund had actually lost −2.4%.

NB The point of this is to show the differential between the best and worst. The actual performance of any fund will vary depending on the time period selected.

Insight

Picking funds can be incredibly difficult as there are so many variables and the best-performing fund last year can sometimes be the worst-performing fund this year. Unless you are comfortable with doing this for yourself, this is an area that is probably best left to a professional adviser, who will be able to select the best fund for your requirements.

Active v passive

A passive fund (which can also be called a tracker fund) will simply attempt to track a particular benchmark, such as the FTSE 100, and provide returns in line with that index. An actively managed fund will attempt to outperform that index or other stated benchmark by picking particular investments that the fund manager believes will lead to better returns.

The advantages of a passive fund are that they are usually cheaper, and you are not dependent on a manager's skill to pick the right investments. The disadvantage is that they may not perform as well as the best performing managed funds and that most of these funds are restricted to a specific asset class. This means you will need several different funds to achieve any level of diversification between asset classes.

Insight

The argument between whether an active fund is better than a passive fund has raged for many years with both sides having their supporters and detractors. The main focus of the argument in favour of a passive fund is that over the longer period of time very few managers outperform the average and there is no guarantee that even those that have will continue to do so. The counter argument is that some funds do consistently outperform the average so they are a better investment. I will often recommend a mixture of both for my clients.

Risk profiles

Different organizations use different definitions of risk and different scales. Some use a scale of 1 to 10, with 1 being low and 10 being high. The profile below has 6 levels and gives some indication of some of the most popular type of funds and what to expect in most circumstances, *although it must be stressed that from time to time exceptions will occur and there can be no guarantee that all investments at all times will perform in line with the explanations given.*

Risk level	Type of savings/ investments	Pros	Cons
1	Deposit accounts	Your money will be very safe. You will usually be able to access your money quickly and easily.	Your money will struggle to keep pace with inflation. The interest may not be sufficient to meet your needs.
2	Fixed interest funds	Over the medium term (4–7 years) you would expect higher returns than deposit accounts.	There will be times when values will fall, although these should be fairly small.
3	Defensive managed funds Cautious managed funds	Over the medium term (4–7 years) you would expect higher returns than deposit accounts or fixed interest funds.	Values will fall from time to time. Usually these will be relatively small but there could be times when falls are higher than expected.

4	Balanced managed funds UK Equity funds	Over the medium to long term (5–10 years) you would expect higher returns than defensive or cautious managed funds.	There will be occasions when falls in value could be substantial but these will tend to be fairly infrequent.
5	Adventurous managed funds US and European funds	Potential to have large gains.	There is a high risk to your capital.
6	Emerging market funds Specialist fund investing in a narrow range such as technology	Potential for very large gains.	Significant risk to your capital and these fund will be very volatile.

TEN POINTS TO REMEMBER

1 There is a difference between the investment wrapper and the investment itself.

2 The term 'wrapper' or 'vehicle' refers to the structure and tax treatment of a product.

3 Before thinking about where to invest you should first consider what your objectives are.

4 There is no such thing as a risk-free investment.

5 When considering risk you need to take into account the risk to your capital overall and the risk of the investment rising and falling along the way.

6 There are four main asset classes: cash, fixed interest, property and equities although some investments do not fall into these classes.

7 One of the most important aspects when investing is not to put all your eggs in one basket.

8 A managed fund will invest in a different number of different asset types and there are a range of different types to chose from.

9 An active fund will be run by a manager who picks the investments, a passive fund will track a single index or series of indices.

10 Even apparently similar funds can have a very different make-up.

10

Investments: deposit accounts and National Savings

In this chapter you will learn about:
- *deposit accounts*
- *cash ISAs*
- *National Savings*

Over the next few chapters we will look at specific savings and investment types in more detail. For each investment we will review aspects such as:

- ▶ *how the investment works*
- ▶ *taxation*
- ▶ *the advantages*
- ▶ *the disadvantages*
- ▶ *things to look out for*
- ▶ *where to get one*
- ▶ *what happens if things go wrong.*

Deposit accounts

Whilst deposit accounts are one of the simplest and most secure forms of investment, even they require a certain number of considerations to be taken into account. For example, over a period of time most will struggle to keep pace with inflation.

HOW DO THEY WORK?

At the risk of stating the obvious, a deposit account works by paying interest on the money you invest. The rate of interest can be fixed for a certain period of time or variable. The main types of deposit account are:

- **Instant access:** *with an instant access account you can withdraw your money on demand. They usually pay the lowest rate of interest.*
- **Notice:** *notice accounts will pay a higher rate of interest than instant access accounts in return for having to give notice to make a withdrawal, say 30 or 90 days. There are a number of variations on the theme, including accounts that will let you take a certain number of withdrawals, say one a month without penalty.*
- **Fixed-term bonds:** *these usually pay an even higher rate of interest in return for you agreeing to tie up your money for a certain period, say 1–3 years.*
- **50+/60+ accounts:** *an increasing number of accounts are being made available to customers over a certain age, typically 50 or 60. The main point of these accounts is that they will usually pay a higher rate of interest than a similar one from the same organization that is available to someone under these ages.*

HOW ARE THEY TAXED?

You pay Income Tax on the interest paid irrespective of whether or not you draw that interest. In the majority of cases basic rate tax will be deducted before the interest is paid. If you are a basic rate taxpayer you will have no further tax to pay. If you are a higher rate taxpayer you will have to pay an additional amount to cover higher rate tax.

If you are a non-taxpayer you will *not* usually be able to reclaim any tax that has been deducted, but you can usually arrange for the interest to be paid without deduction of Income Tax by completing an R85 form that can be obtained from the organization with whom you place the deposit.

Insight

Deposit accounts are nearly always advertised with the gross rate before tax is deducted. In planning your finances you must consider the amount you will receive after tax as this is the amount you will actually receive. For example, if the interest rate is 3%, then as a basic rate taxpayer you will only receive 2.4%. On a deposit of £10,000 this is the difference between £300 a year and £240.

WHAT ARE THE ADVANTAGES?

The main advantage of a deposit account is a very high level of financial security. If you have an instant access account you will be able to access your money without delay. They are also simple to understand and widely available.

WHAT ARE THE DISADVANTAGES?

The main disadvantage of a deposit account is that it may struggle to keep pace with inflation, especially if you take into account the effect of tax. The other disadvantage is that they may not generate sufficient interest to meet your income requirements.

Insight

From about 2000 until about 2007 interest rates were relatively high, but by 2008/9 they had fallen considerably, meaning that it had become difficult to earn an interest rate that would generate a reasonable income. However this hides a fact that may not be immediately obvious, in that there is a very strong relationship between interest rates and inflation. In July 2007, the Bank of England base rate was 5.75% and the retail prices index (RPI) was 3.8%, a difference of 1.95%. By July 2009 the base rate had fallen to 0.5% and RPI was −1.4%, a difference of 1.9%. Whilst there are some exceptions, especially over short periods of time, this differential is remarkably consistent.

THINGS TO LOOK OUT FOR

How often is interest paid?

You need to check how often the interest is actually added to the account. This is especially important if you intend to withdraw the interest regularly, say more than once a year. The frequency with which the interest is added is often different to the rate at which it is earned.

Insight

As well as the best rate, how often interest is added to the account can make a difference to the actual rate of return. For example, if an interest rate of 5% was paid once a year on an investment of £50,000, the interest would be £2,500. If interest was paid daily, based on the same rate of interest, it would produce £2,563.37. Fortunately it is easy enough to make a comparison between these two methods by looking at the Average Equivalent Rate (AER). All savings accounts have to show the AER but it may not always be immediately obvious, with some institutions showing it as a bold headline and others in the 'small print'. In the example given here the second account would have a slightly higher AER than the first.

Changing rates

The next thing to be aware of is that unless you have taken out a deposit with a fixed rate, the rate you are earning can, and often will, change. This means the highly competitive rate you took out a year ago may now be extremely uncompetitive. Many deposit accounts offer an introductory bonus rate (typically 1%) that only lasts for a certain time, say one year. Often this bonus will only be available to new customers.

You may also find that rates are increased at certain times of the year in order to attract new business, only to fall back again a few months later. This often happens in February to April when people are shopping around for ISAs. At this time banks and building societies compete to offer an attractive rate to get new customers through the door.

There are a number of ways you can deal with this, but unfortunately all of them have drawbacks in terms of time or finding out the information that you need.

Probably the most effective way of dealing with this is to monitor the rate you are receiving constantly against the best rate on the market. To constantly get the best deal, this should be done every month and everyone should check their rate at least once a year.

Checking every month doesn't mean moving the account every month, as this is likely to be more trouble in terms of time taken and paperwork completed than it is worth. By checking every month, you will be able to see if the rate you are receiving suddenly plummets.

Insight

For some people, constantly monitoring the interest rate they receive becomes something of an enjoyable habit. However for most of us this will not be the case, but you should check every three months or so. If you only check once a year, my advice is not to do so in February to April when the banks and building societies may raise the rate to attract new business and keep existing customers.

Finally on this point, you need to check the rate you are earning on your existing account is the same as the rate being advertised. Often you will find that the rate being offered is only available to new customers, or is being offered on the series 4 version of the account and you have series 3. Finding this out can be easier said than done, but is worth the effort.

The other way of dealing with the issue of changing rates, is to find an organization that consistently pays an ongoing attractive rate rather than a top rate for a short period of time. The trouble with this strategy is that it can be quite difficult to find the information that you need. Whilst most providers of deposit accounts will publish an interest rate history, to the best of my knowledge there is no table published that allows you to compare this information, meaning that you will have to do a lot of digging for yourself.

As a generalization (and please accept the limitations of any generalization), online providers and smaller building societies tend to be better at offering a reasonable rate on a consistent basis.

Terms and conditions

Equally as important as interest rates are the terms and conditions attaching to the account, in particular any conditions relating to withdrawal and any impact that has on the interest you earn. For example, a few years ago a major bank offered a market leading rate on a deposit account that permitted instant access. However, no interest was payable in any month when a withdrawal was made. This penalty wasn't just on the money withdrawn but on the entire account, so if you had £50,000 in the account and withdrew £1 every month, at the end of the year you wouldn't have earned a penny in interest.

In a similar way if you are investing into an account for a certain period of time, check to see what the conditions are if you need your money back before the end of the period, and do make sure that you are unlikely to need this money, except in totally unforeseen circumstances.

Insight

These points highlight one of the most important issues when saving and investing, or indeed any aspect of dealing with money. Start by deciding what you want, not by looking at what is on offer. If you need or want an account that pays out monthly interest, then you need to look for an account that achieves that and then find the one that pays the highest interest rate.

WHERE TO GET THEM

As well as bank and building society branches, deposit accounts are available online, by post and by phone. Most supermarkets now also offer deposit accounts, often with attractive rates.

If you have internet access then there are a number of websites that will help you find the best rate, but beware most comparison sites charge the organizations they list so not all rates are included.

The FSA also publish comparison tables for deposit accounts. Whilst no charge is made to be included, not all providers will submit their rate. Nonetheless is still worth checking.

Most newspapers will also publish a list of best rates at least weekly.

Rates for internet, telephone or postal accounts tend to be higher than those available 'in branch', but this not always the case.

Also worth researching are something known as affinity accounts. These will be available to you if you are a member of a certain organization or share characteristics with others. Perhaps the best known account of this type is run by SAGA, but these types of accounts are also widely available from motoring organizations, sporting clubs, unions, employment organizations and others. They tend to offer higher than average rates, they may also be available to family members as well as actual members of the organization. These accounts rarely appear on comparison websites or tables, so tracking them down can be fairly difficult, but if you or someone in your family is a member of any form of organization it is always worth checking.

PROTECTION IF THINGS GO WRONG

Events in 2007 and 2008 highlighted the risks of what might have happened to people's money in a deposit account if the organization holding the money failed. Fortunately in the UK, as a result of mergers and government takeovers, the worst didn't happen, but it was a wake-up call for many of us.

As things stand at the moment, the Financial Services Compensation Scheme provides 100% cover for deposit accounts of £50,000 per person per organization. So if you have a joint account then you will have £100,000 protection. One issue with this is that with all the mergers that have occurred, you may have money invested in two or more different organizations, but if both of those organizations are ultimately owned by the same company you may have only one set of protection.

More information on what protection is available can be found on the Financial Services Compensation Scheme (FSCS) website (details for this can be found at the end of this book).

Cash ISAs

Despite what most people think, a cash ISA isn't actually a product at all, but the way a product is taxed. Most, but not all, cash ISAs are simply deposit accounts and as such the points above apply equally to them.

Interest paid under a cash ISA is free of Income Tax and you don't have to declare them on your Income Tax return. Because of this nearly everyone should consider a cash ISA before any other form of saving or investment and a couple should both use their annual ISA allowance.

HOW DO THEY WORK?

Because they are not a product there is no single way an ISA works. They are available in most forms of deposit account, e.g. instant access, notice or fixed term. Every UK resident over the age of 16 can place £5,100 into a cash ISA every year, so it nearly always makes sense to use your allowance every year as over time the amount of tax free interest will build.

> ### *Example*
> Bill and Margaret Smith have £75,000 in a building society deposit account that pays 4%. After tax they receive £2,400 a year in interest. By placing the maximum £5,100 each into an ISA, assuming the same rate of interest, they would receive £2,481.60. Not a vast amount maybe but better in their hands than the tax man. The real difference comes if they continue each year to transfer money to the ISA. Within seven years, assuming the same rate of interest, they would receive £3,000 a year, an extra £600.

THINGS TO LOOK OUT FOR

All the points mentioned in deposit accounts are equally relevant to ISAs, in particular, the issue of rates reducing after you have taken out the product.

National Savings and Investments

Insight

National Savings and Investments (NS&I) aren't really a product but a product provider. The key attraction is that it is backed by HM Treasury (or put another slightly inaccurate way by the government) which make them as secure as anything can be. The product range changes from time to time and up-to-date details can be obtained from the NS&I website or from post offices (details can be found at the back of this book). The section below outlines the main products that you can expect to be available.

PREMIUM BONDS

Probably the most well known NS&I product, Premium Bonds are a monthly prize draw with a £1 million jackpot. The difference between this and the Lottery is that you can always get your stake money back in full.

The advantage of Premium Bonds is that you could win a big prize, the disadvantage is that you may not win anything, but as already mentioned you can get your money back. The main points are:

▶ *minimum investment of £100*
▶ *maximum holding of £30,000*
▶ *winnings are tax free.*

ISA

NS&I provide an ISA that is the same as any other ISA. The rates on NS&I ISAs don't tend to be the best available, but you do have the security of knowing that they are backed by the government.

SAVINGS CERTIFICATES

There are two types of Savings Certificates, fixed interest and index linked. Fixed interest pay a given rate of interest and index linked pay an amount over and above inflation. Both types are issued in batches and run for a certain number of years, typically two, three or five years.

The minimum investment is £100 for both types and you can invest £15,000 per issue. As well as buying new issues, you are allowed to reinvest any maturing certificates without any limit.

If you need your money back, there is no penalty as such for cashing them in before the end of the term but no interest will be paid in the first year and a reduced rate for the remaining years.

Whilst the interest rates on Savings Certificates are not necessarily the best rates you can obtain, they are tax free which means they can be attractive if you compare the net rate with other forms of similar savings, especially if you are a higher rate taxpayer.

GUARANTEED GROWTH BONDS AND GUARANTEED INCOME BONDS

These are similar to Savings Certificates in that they are issued in batches for a fixed period of years; once again one, two, three and five years are the usual periods. They tend to pay a higher rate of interest than Savings Certificates but are not tax free.

As you might expect Growth Bonds are designed to provide capital growth and Income Bonds, income.

Basic rate is deducted at source and if you are a basic rate taxpayer you will have no more tax to pay. If you are a non-taxpayer, you are not able to reclaim the tax and if you are a higher rate taxpayer you will have to pay the difference between basic and higher rate tax.

The only penalty for taking your money out early is 90 days' loss of interest and the minimum holding for each type is £500 and the maximum £1 million.

SAVINGS ACCOUNTS

NS&I also offer savings which work in the same way as any other deposit account. There are two types, one with a passbook and one with a cash card.

WHERE TO BUY THEM

Information on all NS&I Products can by found at the Post Office and you can open some types there as well, although some are only available online, by post or over the phone.

ADVANTAGES

Apart from the government backing, NS&I products are as straightforward and 'catch free' as you can get.

DISADVANTAGES

The only real disadvantage with NS&I products is the rate tends to be lower than other similar products, but as already said they are very secure and catch free.

The other disadvantage, and this applies to all deposit type investments, not just NS&I products, is that they will struggle to keep pace with inflation.

TEN THINGS TO REMEMBER

1 *Deposit accounts are one of the safest types of investment, but they can struggle to keep up with inflation.*

2 *You will usually get a higher rate of interest if you are prepared to tie your money up for a longer period, or from 50+ or 60+ accounts.*

3 *Most deposit accounts will have basic rate tax deducted at source, although you can ask for interest to be paid gross if you are a non-taxpayer.*

4 *The true rate of interest is shown in the Average Equivalent Rate (AER).*

5 *Rates can, and often do, change frequently and the rates advertised might not be the same as you earn on your account.*

6 *Take note of any terms and conditions, such as loss of interest if you make withdrawals.*

7 *If you invest in a cash ISA, interest will be paid tax free.*

8 *You are protected for deposits of up to £50,000 per person per organization.*

9 *National Savings are extremely secure as they are backed by the government.*

10 *Some National Savings products are tax free.*

11

Collective investments

In this chapter you will learn about:
- *Unit Trusts and OEICs*
- *Investment Trusts*
- *Investment Bonds*

A collective investment is a way of gaining access to a much wider range of investments than would be available to most individuals. As well as a good way of obtaining diversification, most forms 'subcontract' the day-to-day investment decisions to a professional investment manager.

Insight

Many people dismiss Unit Trusts and similar investments as being too risky, but a Unit Trust is only the investment wrapper and, as has already been pointed out, this only refers to the structure and tax treatment of the investment. Whether or not an investment is risky depends on where your money is invested. We refer to the actual investment as the 'underlying investment' or fund.

Unit Trusts and OEICs

A Unit Trust and OEIC (OEIC stands for Open-Ended Investment Company), are essentially the same thing, the only difference being some technicalities and legal structure. A Unit Trust can only be sold in the UK whereas an OEIC can be sold throughout the EU, which is why they are gradually taking over from Unit Trusts.

In August 2009 members of the Investment Managers Association (the IMA is the main UK trade body for these funds) offered 2,394 funds in 30 different categories, or as the IMA calls them Sector Classifications, covering everything from Protected/Guaranteed Funds to a sector covering Global Emerging Markets.

Even though each sector covers funds that invest in similar assets and geographic areas, there can still be a considerable difference in the actual investments made between funds in the same sector.

> The expression 'Unit Trust' or 'OEIC' refers to the legal structure of the investment, the expression 'fund' is used to indicate where the money is invested. For example, you can invest in a UK Equity Fund OEIC which means that the investment is in UK company shares and the legal structure is an OEIC.

HOW DO THEY WORK?

The fund is divided into a number of units or, in the case of OEICs, shares. A fund may be worth £1 million and have 1 million £1 units. As the fund rises or falls in value so does the price of the units. If the value of the fund rose to £2 million, each unit would be worth £2, and if the value of the fund fell to £500,000, each unit would be worth 50p.

When you invest you buy units in the fund. These are not existing units as extra units are created when your money is added to the pool of money that is invested. When you want to take money out of the fund then you encash your units and the fund manager will send you a cheque or more probably credit your bank account.

Example

Mary Rogers invested £25,000 in a Unit Trust. At that time each unit was worth 85 pence so she bought 29,411.76 units. When she came to sell the units five years later, each unit was worth £1.19 so her investment was worth £34,999.99, i.e. £1.19 × 29,411.76 units.

Most funds offer the choice of income or accumulation units. Income units are used if you want to draw off the income from the fund and accumulation if you want capital growth. You will usually choose at the outset which type you want and it is usually possible to have a mixture of both. Even if you have income units but do not want to draw an income, then it is perfectly possible to reinvest the income directly back into the fund for capital growth.

FUND PLATFORMS

Traditionally one of the problems with Unit Trusts and OEICs was that if you wanted to move from a fund offered by one fund company to a fund offered by a different company, then you would have to sell your units in the first company, wait for your cheque and then invest in the second. In practice this was relatively straightforward but it took time and, more importantly, could be costly as every time you invested in the new company you would incur new set-up charges.

To overcome this problem something known as 'fund platforms' were created. These work by enabling you to access a wide range of funds (sometimes over 1,000) through one organization. Usually there is no additional charge for this as the companies that offer these platforms make their money by charging you the same price as it would cost to invest directly with the fund manger, but obtain a discount from that fund manager.

The advantage of a fund platform is that you can have a wide range of funds but only one set of paperwork. Just as importantly, it is easy to change funds (usually for a nominal cost), either online or by phone.

Insight

This ability to change funds easily can be important for a number of reasons. You may wish to move from one type of fund to another in order to increase or reduce your investment risk, or to reflect other changes in your

(Contd)

requirements. You may also want to change your fund manager if they start to underperform. Finally, changing funds can be a great way of keeping any tax you may pay on profit to a minimum as doing this counts as a disposal for Capital Gains Tax.

WHAT DO THEY COST?

Although the way charges are levied vary, nearly all can be broken down into two main types. Nearly every fund will charge a set-up fee known as an initial charge. Whilst this charge varies, a typical cost is 5% of the amount invested.

On top of this there will be an ongoing charge known as the Annual Management Charge (AMC). Once again this varies but anything over 1%–1.5% would need to be justified by a proven track record of above average performance.

Certain costs of running the fund also will be passed on to you and these costs are added to the annual management charge to give what is known as the Total Expense Ratio (TER).

Whilst this may seem rather complex, the good news is that all of these charges are shown in a document known as a Key Features Document (KFD).

As well as showing the individual charges, a Key Features Document has to show the combined impact of these charges based on certain assumed returns, usually 6% or, if the investment is placed in an ISA, 7%. This enables you to see the impact the charges will have on your returns over set periods, typically ten years, although other timescales may be shown as well. So if the assumed rate of return without any charges was 6% a year, and the impact of the charges over ten years added up to 2% a year, your return would be 4%.

Insight
It is vital to understand the projected returns used in Key Features Documents are not estimates of what the returns

from the fund might be. They only show the impact of the charges if the return was that stated in the document. They serve no other purpose and you should be aware that the very best and very worst performing funds have to use the same assumed returns for this purpose.

High charges don't necessarily mean better performance, although many of the funds that consistently outperform the average will have higher than average charges, but so do some of the worst. On the other hand very low charges are of no benefit if the returns are poor. After all, 0% of £1 million is still nothing. What this means is that although charges are a factor in selecting a fund they shouldn't be the only one used.

TAXATION

Generally speaking any income from a Unit Trust or OEIC is subject to Income Tax and gains are subject to Capital Gains Tax, although the precise detail will depend on the type of investment. Every year you will receive a statement showing you how much income has been received and when you sell your fund you will receive a statement showing how much gain (or loss) you have made.

Income from dividends received by the fund are subject to Income Tax. This tax is deducted at source and as a basic rate taxpayer you will have no further tax to pay. A non-taxpayer cannot recover this tax and a higher rate taxpayer will have to pay the difference between basic rate and higher rate tax.

Income from interest is also subject to Income Tax. Once again this will be deducted at source and a basic rate taxpayer will have no further liability and a higher rate taxpayer has to pay the difference between basic and higher rate. The difference to dividend income is that if you are not a taxpayer, then usually you will be able to reclaim this tax.

An important point to note is that even if you do not draw the income the tax is still payable, but this is also true of a deposit account.

UK-based Unit Trusts and OEICs don't pay Capital Gains Tax (CGT), but you may personally be liable for any gain that you make from the fund. Any gains may be subject to CGT. Whether they actually are or not depends on two factors:

▶ *the type of fund*
▶ *whether a gain is made.*

Whether gains could be subject to CGT will depend on where the fund invests. Many fixed interest funds such as UK gilt and Corporate Bond funds are not subject to CGT at all. The best way of checking whether or not CGT may be payable is to ask the fund manager or look in the section of the Key Features Document headed Taxation which will explicitly state if CGT may be payable. In the vast majority of circumstances you have to be provided with this document before you invest.

Even if a gain occurs in a fund where a liability to Capital Gains Tax may arise, whether any tax actually has to be paid will depend on your personal situation.

Insight

Capital Gains Tax is widely misunderstood and many people shy away from investments that may be subject to this tax fearing that they could have an extremely large tax bill. In fact, in many situations the opposite is true and selecting an investment that may be subject to Capital Gains Tax can often minimize the amount of tax that has to be paid. Even if Capital Gains Tax is payable, the rate is lower than Income Tax.

ADVANTAGES OF UNIT TRUSTS AND OEICS

The advantages of Unit Trusts and OEICs are:

▶ *There is an enormous choice of investments, meaning that there is something available for most people.*

> - *It is very easy to change investment strategy, especially if arranged through a 'platform'. For example, if you are investing for ten years you may want to start out being fairly adventurous and as you get nearer to the end of your timescale switch to a more cautious investment in order to reduce the risk and preserve any profits that you have made to date.*
> - *They can be highly tax efficient.*
> - *There is no minimum or maximum timescale for the investment. This means that you could put your money in today and take it out tomorrow*, although most advisers recommend a minimum timescale of five years or more in order to maximize the chance of 'riding out' any falls in value.*

*Some funds, mainly property funds, have the right to impose what they call a moratorium which means they could require you to wait a certain period, say six months, before you can access your money. The reason for this is that if a lot of people want their money out of the fund at the same time, the fund may have to sell some properties in order to meet that demand. If you have ever tried to sell a house you will know how long that can take, so imagine how much more difficult and time-consuming it would be to sell several multimillion-pound office blocks or retail parks, especially in a recession.

DISADVANTAGES OF UNIT TRUSTS AND OEICS

The main disadvantages are:

> - *The range of choice means it can be difficult to pick the right one for your personal circumstances.*
> - *Although some protected and guaranteed investments exist, in most cases there will be no guarantee that you will make a profit or even get your money back.*
> - *They can be complicated from a tax point of view, in the sense that you may need to enter details on a tax return.*
> - *You may need to pay tax on income, even if the capital value of the fund has fallen.*

There are a number of ways to invest in a Unit Trust or an OEIC:

▶ *directly with the Unit Trust/OEIC provider*
▶ *through a fund platform*
▶ *through an intermediary.*

Buying directly

You can approach the Unit Trust/OEIC provider directly and they will provide you with the forms you need to invest. Usually you will then complete the forms and return them with a cheque. Alternatively you can often apply online or by phone. The disadvantage of this approach is that you will only be able to choose from the funds provided by that manager. If you want to change funds at any time there may not be something suitable in that manager's range. Perhaps more importantly you have to decide which fund is right for you and you will have no comeback if you make the wrong choice.

Buying through a platform or funds supermarket

The procedure for this is the same as buying directly and the advantage is that you will have a wide range of funds and providers to choose from. It will usually be relatively easy to switch funds if that becomes desirable. Usually the cost will be the same as buying directly from a Unit Trust/OEIC provider. Once again these fund supermarkets will not provide any advice so you are on your own when it comes to choosing the right fund or funds.

Buying through an intermediary

This subdivides into three main groups:

▶ *those that sell their own or a limited range of funds*
▶ *independent advisers*
▶ *discount brokers.*

The first group includes most banks and building societies. Whilst the range of funds and providers are limited they will usually do all the administration of setting up the investment for you. Furthermore, provided they deal with you on what is known as an advised basis they have a responsibility to ensure the product they recommend is suitable for your needs. In terms of costs, the adviser will usually be paid by commission on the product that they sell to you.

Independent advisers have access to many different providers and as such not only have to find the most suitable fund for you but also the most suitable provider. They may charge you a fee for the advice, or with your permission, take commission from the provider whose product they recommend.

Insight

Be wary if either of these two types of intermediary arranges an investment for you on a 'non-advised' or 'execution only' basis. These terms mean that the intermediary hasn't advised you in any way and you take full responsibility for ensuring the investment is suitable for your needs.

Discount brokers are generally found online and also have access to a wide choice of providers. They are also independent in the sense that they are not tied to a single or small group of providers. Usually they are cheaper than the other methods described but they won't provide you with any advice.

THINGS TO WATCH OUT FOR

With over 2,000 different funds to choose from, the biggest issue when investing in a Unit Trust or an OEIC is selecting which one is right for you. The key thing, whether you invest directly or through an intermediary, is to ensure you understand the risk attached to the investment fully. The key questions to ask are:

▶ *What is the minimum timescale I should be thinking about for this investment?*
▶ *How much is the investment likely to rise and fall during the time I hold it?*

- ▶ *What is the risk to my capital?*
- ▶ *What tax may I have to pay?*
- ▶ *What are the charges?*
- ▶ *What are the terms and conditions?*
- ▶ *How well has the fund performed?*

Insight

The last point warrants further explanation. Without a crystal ball it is impossible to know how well a particular fund will perform. There are a number of factors you can look at, including how well the fund has performed in the past but this can hide a multitude of sins. Even in the same sector, a fund may have performed well because it is more adventurous or below average because it is more cautious. Therefore unless you feel you have sufficient knowledge to pick a suitable fund, this may be an area where you will want to seek advice.

PROTECTION IF THINGS GO WRONG

The way money is held in a unit trust or an OEIC means that if the organization fails, your money will usually be protected. If the worst happens and this is not the case, protection will usually be provided by the FSCS up to £50,000. You should check the key features document for confirmation that the particular investment you are buying is covered in this way.

Investment Trusts

These share many of the characteristics of Unit Trusts and OEICs, for example, they are collective investments that use the services of a professional fund manager and are taxed in the same way.

WHAT ARE THEY?

An Investment Trust is a limited company. Like all companies they issue shares and the shareholders own that company. Therefore if you invest in an Investment Trust, what you are actually doing is buying a share of a company in the same way you would if you bought a share in any company.

The difference between an Investment Trust and other companies is that they don't make or sell anything. Instead they invest in other companies by buying other companies' shares.

In this respect they are similar to a Unit Trust or an OEIC but they differ in the following ways:

Unit Trust/OEIC	Investment Trust
The number of units or shares increases or decreases whenever anyone invests or disinvests.	The number of shares are fixed.
In the main they cannot borrow money.	They can and often do borrow money.
The value of the units are directly related to the value of the fund.	The value of the shares are dependent on what someone will pay for them.

This last point is best explained by way of an example. If the value of a Unit Trust or OEIC fund is £1,000,000 and there are 1,000,000 units, each unit will be worth £1. In an Investment Trust with investments valued at £1,000,000 and 1,000,000 shares, each share could be more or less than £1.

Like all companies, the value of an Investment Trust's shares will not only reflect the value of the investments made by the Investment Trust but also whether investors think the company's shares will rise or fall in the future.

Like Unit Trusts and OEICs, there is a wide choice of funds and providers to choose from.

What are the advantages over Unit Trusts and OEICs?
Investment Trusts tend to have lower charges than Unit Trusts and OEICs and, because they can borrow money to make investments

and shares, can be worth more than the value of the investments they offer the opportunity for higher returns.

What are the disadvantages compared to Unit Trusts and OEICs?
If an Investment Trust made exactly the same investments as a Unit Trust or OEIC it would be considered to be a higher risk investment for exactly the same reasons as given for the opportunities for higher returns, i.e. it can borrow money to invest and the shares can be worth more or less than the underlying investments.

TAXATION

The tax treatment of Investment Trusts is broadly the same as for Unit Trusts, i.e. income will be subject to Income Tax and capital gains subject to Capital Gains Tax.

PROTECTION IF THINGS GO WRONG

Most UK-based Investment Trusts will be protected by the FSCS in the same way as Unit Trusts and OEICs. However, before investing in a specific Investment Trust you should check that this is the case and the level of cover provided.

Insight

Because they can borrow in order to invest and because the shares can be worth more or less than the actual investments held by the trust, I consider that Investment Trusts are really only for experienced investors and/or a small proportion of your overall capital.

Insurance/Investment Bonds

As has been stated before, the word 'bond' is an overused word when it comes to money, describing many different types of savings and investments.

In this instance it refers to a specific product that is in many ways a direct competitor to Unit Trusts and OEICs. They can still be a useful investment in certain circumstances, for example they can be a useful vehicle for deferring tax and in some instances will not be taken into account for some state benefits such as nursing home fees.

> Insurance and Investment Bond are alternative names for the same product, although for the rest of this section I will just refer to them as Investment Bonds.

HOW DO THEY WORK?

In terms of actual investment they work pretty much in the same way as a Unit Trust or OEIC, namely, they offer:

- ▶ *A wide range of investments covering a wide range of risk.*
- ▶ *Normally there is no maximum or minimum investment term.*
- ▶ *The amount you get back will depend on how well the investment performs.*

In fact, exactly the same investment fund is often available through an Unit Trust/OEIC and Investment Bond. The major difference between the two types of investment is the way an Investment Bond is taxed which, depending on your circumstances, could work either for you or against you.

HOW IS AN INVESTMENT BOND TAXED?

Technically an Investment Bond is a life assurance policy which means that it is only subject to Income Tax. At first glance this may appear advantageous when compared with a Unit Trust/OEIC, which may be subject to Income Tax and Capital Gains Tax, but more often than not this not the case.

Whilst generally speaking you will have to pay Income Tax on income from a Unit Trust/OEIC, and Capital Gains Tax on any gain, with an Investment Bond Income Tax has to be paid on both income and gains.

Unlike a Unit Trust/OEIC, the Income Tax is payable by the fund itself before any income or profit is paid out. The main advantage of this is that if you are a basic rate taxpayer your tax affairs are much easier to administer. The main disadvantage is that whilst most people use their personal Income Tax allowance (your Personal Allowance is the income you receive that is not liable to Income Tax) the vast majority of people do not use their Capital Gains Tax allowance.

Example

Fred Aston invests £50,000 in an Investment Bond and his wife Flo also invests £50,000 on the same day in a Unit Trust. Both invest in exactly the same underlying fund, in other words their money is ultimately invested in exactly the same place. The fund grows at 5% a year for five years. At the end of the five years, Fred will receive £60,832.65. As a basic rate taxpayer Fred will not have any further tax to pay as it has already been deducted from the fund. Flo will receive £63,814 but she will have to pay some Capital Gains Tax on this money. At the time of writing she will have to pay £668.53 in Capital Gains Tax, but that still leaves her £2,312.82 better off.

The example above ignores any difference in charges between the two products and in practice, due to the complex way Investment Bonds pay tax, Fred's return would probably have been a little higher.

If Flo switched funds before the gain exceeded her Capital Gains Tax allowance, she might not have had to pay any Capital Gains Tax at all.

The way tax is actually dealt with depends on the rate of tax you actually pay when you cash in the bond.

Any profit the bond has made is divided by the number of complete years you have held the bond and the resultant figure is added to your taxable income for the year. This process of dividing the total profit by the number of years you have held the bond is known as top slicing.

If the two figures added together mean that you won't pay any Income Tax then you will have no tax to pay, but you will not be able to reclaim the tax already paid within the fund.

If the two figures added together do not exceed the basic rate tax band then you will not have any further tax to pay, as it is deemed that the tax liability has been paid from the fund.

If the two figures added together take you into the higher rate tax band, then you will have to pay the difference between the higher and basic rate of tax.

The other point to consider is the potential impact on Age Allowance. If you recall, anyone over the age of 65 with income up to a certain level is entitled to an additional allowance on their income before they have to pay tax. This additional allowance is called the Age Allowance.

When the profit is taken from an Investment Bond, this is added to a person's other income in the tax year that they encash the bond. In this instance the profit is not top sliced and if the total exceeds the threshold level for the Age Allowance it will be reduced or in some case could be removed altogether.

Insight

If you invested in an Investment Bond through an adviser you have every right to expect them to calculate the tax implications of the product they are recommending. To avoid any doubt it is always worth asking, 'What tax will I have to pay and what, if any, is the likely impact on my Age

(Contd)

Allowance?' Make sure you get the reply in writing. If you have arranged the investment for yourself or you haven't received advice then you will have to calculate the tax consequences for yourself or pay someone to do it for you.

'INCOME' FROM AN INVESTMENT BOND

Insight

One way Investment Bonds are sold is on the basis that you can take 5% tax-free income every year. As explained below this is highly misleading, as the 5% is not income nor is it tax free.

One of the attractions of Investment Bonds is that you can withdraw up to 5% each year without an immediate liability to tax and this is the basis for the statement referred to above. However, this withdrawal is *not* income, it is 5% of the amount that you invested in the first place. In other words, if the bond didn't make any profit then after 20 years you wouldn't have any money left. Hopefully this situation won't happen and the bond will make a profit. However the withdrawals you have taken are added back into the equation when you cash in the bond to see if you have any tax to pay and whether there will be any impact on your Age Allowance.

Example

Gary invested £50,000 in an Investment Bond and withdrew 5%, i.e. £2,500 a year for ten years. After ten years he decided to cash in the bond when it was worth £70,000. The figure that will be used to calculate if he has any tax to pay will be £45,000, i.e. £20,000 being the difference between the £50,000 he invested and the £70,000 value when he cashed it in, plus the 10 x £2,500 that he withdrew every year.

This doesn't mean you pay any more tax than you otherwise would, and in fact being able to put off paying any potential tax liability can often be a benefit, although bear in mind that basic rate tax is being deducted from the fund on an annual basis before any profit is added to your investment.

WHAT ARE THE ADVANTAGES OF INVESTMENT BONDS?

The main advantages of Investment Bonds are:

▶ *A wide range of investments are available matching most risk attitudes.*
▶ *For most basic rate taxpayers the tax treatment is reasonably straightforward.*
▶ *Most are subdivided into a series of sub-plans.*
▶ *They offer the opportunity to defer any tax liability.*
▶ *You can withdraw 5% every year without an immediate liability to tax.*
▶ *If you die they will pay out at least the amount invested less any withdrawals made.*
▶ *They may not be taken into account for nursing care benefits.*

These points are explained in more detail below.

A wide range of investments are available matching most risk attitudes

Not so many years ago, the investment choice for these bonds was extremely limited. Now most providers have a wide choice of funds meaning most people will be able to select a fund in line with their attitude to investment risk. Furthermore, most providers will allow you to select more than one fund and switch between funds without a charge.

For most basic rate taxpayers the tax treatment is reasonably straightforward

Provided the profit from the bond means you remain within the basic tax limit and it doesn't impact on your Age Allowance, there are no tax complications or extensive returns to complete as the tax is automatically deducted from the fund and you have no further tax to pay.

Most are subdivided into a series of sub-plans

Most providers divide their Investment Bonds into a number, typically 100, separate bonds known as segments. This doesn't mean you will get 100 separate documents; you will only get one. Dividing the bonds up in this way has several advantages if you only want to cash in part of your bond as you can encash as many segments as you need without having to encash the entire bond.

It is very important from a tax point of view to encash entire segments and not partial segments, as due to the peculiar way partial encashments are treated for tax you could end up with a tax bill even if the bond has fallen in value.

They offer the opportunity to defer any tax liability
Unless you withdraw more than 5% from your bond in a year, any additional tax due is paid when you encash the bond. This can be useful if you are a higher rate taxpayer when you take the bond out but only a basic rate taxpayer when you cash it in.

If you die they will pay out at least the amount invested less any withdrawals made
On death an Investment Bond will pay the higher of, slightly more (usually 101%) than the amount originally invested, or the current value of the bond.

This is an advantage over a Unit Trust/OEIC or an Investment Trust where the amount on death will be the value of the fund at the date of death, so if the fund has fallen the amount payable on death could be less than the amount invested.

They may not be taken into account for nursing care benefits
Technically an Investment Bond is a life assurance and as such its value shouldn't be taken into account when assessing the capital a person has to ascertain if they are eligible for state benefits such as nursing care.

However, as you may expect the rules on this are rather complex and if it can be proven that you have taken out one of these bonds so your capital won't be taken into account for this benefit, then it will be included in any entitlement to benefit assessment.

More often than not the biggest issue in this situation is convincing the local authority that the Investment Bond shouldn't be included.

WHAT ARE THE DISADVANTAGES OF INVESTMENT BONDS?

The main disadvantages of Investment Bonds are:

- ▶ *If you are a non-taxpayer you cannot recover the tax that is deducted from the fund.*
- ▶ *Most people use their personal Income Tax allowance every year meaning they have to pay tax on all of the investment.*
- ▶ *There are often penalties for taking your money out within a certain period.*
- ▶ *The charges tend to be more complicated than a Unit Trust or an OEIC.*
- ▶ *The tax treatment can sometimes be complex.*

If you are a non-taxpayer you cannot recover the tax that is deducted from the fund

This means you will have paid tax unnecessarily on your investment and, unlike deposit accounts, you can't ask for the tax not to be deducted at source. This will often mean that an Investment Bond is unsuitable for a non-taxpayer.

Most people use their personal Income Tax allowance every year meaning they have to pay tax on all of the investment

An Investment Bond is subject to Income Tax on both the income the fund receives and any capital growth. If you are a basic rate taxpayer you will not normally have to pay any more tax, but the tax has still been paid effectively reducing the amount the fund will have grown.

This compares unfavourably with a Unit Trust or OEIC where the growth will usually be subject to Capital Gains Tax. At the time of writing Capital Gains Tax is 18% compared with 20% for basic rate Income Tax or 40% for higher rate. Whilst these rates may change, Capital Gains Tax is usually charged at a lower rate then Income Tax.

Furthermore, everyone has an allowance for Capital Gains Tax as well as an allowance for Income Tax which means that the first part of any gain (or put another way profit) is not taxed.

> ### Insight
> Very few people use their Capital Gains Tax allowance whereas nearly everyone uses at least some of their Income Tax allowance. This means that for most people a Unit Trust/OEIC will be more tax efficient than an Investment Bond.

There are often penalties for taking your money out within a certain period

Most Investment Bonds will impose a penalty if you want to access your money within a certain period, say five years. This penalty will usually be on a sliding scale reducing over time.

The charges tend to be more complicated than a Unit Trust or an OEIC

In some ways the fact that the charges are more complicated than a Unit Trust or an OEIC is irrelevant as in most circumstances before you invest you will be provided with a Key Features Document (KFD) that sets out the most important points about the investment, including the charges.

In the same way as a Unit Trust/OEIC, one of the items in this document is a statement that shows the impact of the charges at a certain growth rate. For example, it may show the impact of the charges at 6% is 2% which means that if the fund itself after tax grows at 6%, the impact of the charges would mean you would only receive 4%.

Most Investment Bonds look as if they will invest more than you have paid in, and in this way the charging structure can appear misleading. The actual amount will vary according to the company and amount you invest, but figures in the range of 101% to 105% are very common. On the face of it this looks very attractive but most Investment Bonds also have a charge known as the 'bid–offer' spread.

The bid–offer spread refers to the difference in price between the amount you have to pay for your investment and the price you will receive when you cash it in. The amount of the bid–offer spread varies but is usually around 5%. This means the apparently generous initial investment terms are usually clawed back in some shape or form.

Insight

There is nothing wrong with the fact that there are a number of different charges relating to this product or even the fact that there is a bid–offer spread, but what is wrong in my opinion is that it appears the amount invested is more than the amount you place into the bond, when in nearly all cases the additional amount will be clawed back later.

The tax treatment can sometimes be complex

If the top-sliced profit from a bond takes you into the higher rate tax band or the entire profit means that your Age Allowance is reduced, then working out how much tax to pay can become complex.

Also, if you partially surrender a bond then due to the way the tax is calculated you could be faced with a tax bill even if the bond has made a loss.

With-Profit Bonds

A With-Profit Bond is an Investment Bond but one in which your money is specifically invested. Sometimes it will be one of a wide range of funds on offer and sometimes it will be the only fund.

Apart from where the money is actually invested, all other aspects of a With-Profit Bond are exactly the same as any other Investment Bond, but because they are often marketed as a stand alone product it is worth taking a little time to explain how With-Profits Bonds work.

A With-Profits fund invests in a variety of different investments, for example, stocks and shares, fixed interest investments, cash and property. The balance between these investments varies between company to company and will vary from time to time. In this respect a With-Profits fund is not really any different to many other forms of managed fund. The key difference is that the fund manager will hold some of the investment profit back in the good years and use that money to bolster payments in the bad. This is called 'smoothing'.

How this smoothed profit is passed on to you varies, but it will usually be in the form of a bonus. Some bonuses once given can't be taken away, although more often than not they are not payable at once but on a given date in the future. If you encash the policy before the agreed date the bonus can and often will be reduced. This type of bonus is known as an annual bonus or by its more traditional name, reversionary bonus.

The other type of bonus is paid when you encash the plan and is known as a final or terminal bonus. The product provider will change this from time to time depending on how much money is in the fund. When investment times are good it will tend to be higher than when they are bad. Unlike the annual bonus, the amount can literally change overnight or even be withdrawn altogether.

Insight

Theoretically With-Profits are a fantastic idea. The actual investment is usually a good balanced mix and the smoothing out of the peaks and troughs of investing is a very attractive idea. In the past this worked very well as the bulk of the bonus came from the annual bonus, which provided you kept the plan to the agreed date, couldn't be taken away. I still think they are a great idea in theory and many older plans are worth keeping but I will only ever recommend a new With-Profits investment in the rarest of circumstances, as often a significant amount of any profit will tend to come from the final bonus which can be taken away at a moment's notice.

Unit Trusts/OEICs v Investment Trusts v Investment Bonds

Insight

Given that you have a similar choice, and in some cases exactly the same choice, as to where your money is invested, the question then arises as to which investment wrapper is best. The table on pages 194–6 shows the three types side by side including the pros and cons. The truth is that each has its place. There is no absolute right answer and each type will be the most suited in most circumstances.

Because Investment Trusts can borrow money to invest and the value of shares is not directly linked to the value of the investments it holds, it offers the opportunity for the greatest return but also the highest risk which means that they are only usually suitable for experienced investors.

This leaves Unit Trust/OEICs and Investment Bonds as the only real difference between them is the tax treatment. Given that most people use their Income Tax allowance but don't use their Capital Gains Tax allowance, then Unit Trusts/OEICs will tend to give a higher return than Investment Bonds for the same investment.

Nevertheless, below is a list of questions you will to be able to answer before making a final selection.

1 *Why is the particular fund right for you?*
2 *Why have you selected a Unit Trust or OEIC/Investment Trust/Investment Bond over the other types of investments?*
3 *What are the charges on the product compared with the alternatives?*
4 *What are the advantages from a taxation point of view of your recommendation when compared with the alternatives?*
5 *How will the tax treatment affect your Age Allowance? This is only relevant if you are over 65 or will be over 65 by the time you intend to encash the plan.*
6 *What are the penalties, costs and risks if you need your money back earlier than intended?*

	Unit Trust/OEIC	Investment Trust	Investment Bond
Investment choice	A wide choice is available covering many types of investment.	A wide choice is available covering many types of investment.	A wide choice is available covering many types of investment.
How is value measured?	Each unit will have a value; the value of the unit will rise and fall in line with the value of the underlying assets.	The value of the shares will depend on a number of factors including the demand for them.	Each unit will have a value; the value of the unit will rise and fall in line with the value of the underlying assets.
How many shares or units are issued?	Every time contributions are made or withdrawn from the fund the number of units increases or decreases.	There are a fixed number of shares.	Every time contributions are made or withdrawn from the fund the number of units increases or decreases.
Tax treatment	Growth will usually be subject to Capital Gains Tax, income to Income Tax.	Growth will usually be subject to Capital Gains Tax, income to Income Tax.	Growth and income are subject to Income Tax.

How is tax actually paid on income?	Basic rate tax is usually deducted at source and you have no further liability. If you are a higher rate taxpayer you will need to pay the difference between basic and higher rate tax.	Basic rate tax is usually deducted at source and you have no further liability. If you are a higher rate taxpayer you will need to pay the difference between basic and higher rate tax.	Where 'true' income is paid it is usually deducted at source and you have no further liability. If you are a higher rate taxpayer you will need to pay the difference between basic and higher rate tax. [2]
How is tax paid on any gains?	Any Capital Gains Tax has to be paid by you following a 'chargeable event'. [1]	Any Capital Gains Tax has to be paid by you following a 'chargeable event'. [1]	Basic rate Income Tax is paid within the fund. Any liability for higher rate tax has to be paid by you.
What are the main advantages?	More favourable tax treatment than Investment Bond for most people. No fixed term. Rarely any penalties for early encashment. Value directly reflects underlying assets.	More favourable tax treatment than Investment Bond for most people. No fixed term. Rarely any penalties for early encashment. Opportunity for growth greater than underlying assets.	Provided no issues for higher rate tax, administration of tax relatively straightforward. Ability to draw 5% capital each year with no immediate liability to tax. May not be taken into account when assessing capital for some state benefits.

(Contd)

	Unit Trust/OEIC	Investment Trust	Investment Bond
What are the main disadvantages?	Administration of tax can be more complex than Investment Bond. Can be liable for Income Tax on income even if capital value has fallen.	Administration of tax can be more complex than Investment Bond. Can be liable for Income Tax on income even if capital value has fallen.	Tax treatment means growth and will be subject to income tax. Tax can be complex if taken into higher rate tax. Tax may be payable on partial surrender even if a loss is made. Can impact on Age Allowance. Charges can be misleading.

[1] A 'chargeable event' is the technical term used for assessing when a potential liability for tax occurred, in most case this will be when the plan is encashed. Any tax has to be paid in the January following the tax year that the chargeable event occurred. A chargeable event doesn't necessarily mean tax is actually due, just an event has occurred where it may be.

[2] Some Investment Bonds will pay out genuine income based on the income the fund has received. Not all bonds do this and you will need to request for the income to be paid out, usually when you take out the bond. However more often than not the 'income' is not income at all but a withdrawal of capital which is why you will normally see the word income in inverted commas.

TEN POINTS TO REMEMBER

1 *A collective investment is a way of spreading your investment along with lots of other people and using a professional fund manager to make the day-to-day investment decisions.*

2 *There are literally thousands of funds to choose from, which means there is something to align with most people's attitude to risk, but the sheer number makes picking the right one difficult.*

3 *Fund platforms (also sometimes referred to as supermarkets) exist that give you access to a wide range of funds though a single source.*

4 *Income from a Unit Trust/OEIC and Investment Trusts are subject to Income Tax, and gains are usually subject to Capital Gains Tax.*

5 *Income and gains in an Investment Bond are subject to Income Tax with basic rate tax being paid within the fund.*

6 *The main advantages of a Unit Trust/OEIC are:*
  ▷ *There is a wide choice of funds.*
  ▷ *If invested through a fund platform it is easy to change investment strategy.*
  ▷ *They can be tax efficient.*
  ▷ *There is no minimum timescale.*

7 *The main disadvantages of a Unit Trust/OEIC are:*
  ▷ *The range of choice can make picking the right one difficult.*
  ▷ *You will need to enter details on your tax return and have to personally pay any Capital Gains Tax.*
  ▷ *You may have to pay tax on income even if the fund has fallen in value.*

8 *The main advantages of an Investment Bond are:*

▷ *A wide range of investments are available matching most risk attitudes.*

▷ *For most basic rate taxpayers the tax treatment is reasonably straightforward.*

▷ *Most are subdivided into a series of sub-plans.*

▷ *They offer the opportunity to defer any tax liability.*

▷ *You can withdraw 5% every year with an immediate liability to tax.*

▷ *If you die they will pay out at least the amount invested less any withdrawals made.*

▷ *They may not be taken into account for nursing care benefits.*

9 *The main disadvantages of an Investment Bond are:*

▷ *If you are a non-taxpayer you cannot recover the tax that is deducted from the fund.*

▷ *Most people use their personal Income Tax allowance every year meaning they have to pay tax on all of the investment.*

▷ *There are often penalties for taking your money out within a certain period.*

▷ *The charges tend to be more complicated than a Unit Trust or an OEIC.*

▷ *The tax treatment can sometimes be complex, especially if it takes you into higher rate tax or you partially encash a bond.*

10 *Choosing the right underlying investment for your particular circumstances is more important than the investment wrapper.*

Investments: pensions and annuities

In this chapter you will learn about:
- *buying a guaranteed income for life*
- *when investing in a pension may be suitable close to or at retirement*
- *annuities*

An annuity is a way of securing an income in exchange for a lump sum. In fact, when you draw benefits from a personal pension you will usually buy an annuity. In this chapter we will investigate the non-pension version of an annuity.

We will also consider investing in a pension. Covering this in a book aimed at people who are more likely to have already drawn or are about to draw their pensions may seem a little strange, but there are some circumstances where it makes sense to at least consider it.

Pensions

HOW DOES A PENSION WORK?

How pensions work has already been covered in previous chapters, but it is worth repeating a few words here. At this stage the type of pension under consideration is a personal pension which falls within the defined contribution category.

This type of pension works by you investing a sum of money either on a regular basis or as a lump sum. In the vast majority of cases you will be eligible for tax relief on contributions. The money is invested, grows largely free of any tax and when you come to take the benefits you can take up 25% as a tax-free lump sum and the rest as an income for life.

Insight

I fully appreciate that the reputation of pensions has suffered greatly over the last few years and the thought of investing in one may fill you with horror, but please stick with me a little longer. The reason for using a pension is to take advantage of the tax rules, not to make a risky investment. There are pensions available that fit this criteria and this will be covered a little later.

WHEN MAY A PENSION BE SUITABLE CLOSE TO OR AT RETIREMENT?

There are two situations where investing in a pension close to or at retirement may be worth considering and these are:

▶ *where you have already taken benefits from a pension but don't need the income yet*
▶ *where you want to buy an income with a lump sum.*

The first situation can arise if you have left a job that had a pension with it and that pension has started already, or you have drawn a personal pension at the original date it was due to be paid and you don't need or want that income, perhaps because you are still working. Alternatively you may have taken the benefits from a personal pension, perhaps to release the tax-free lump sum, but once again don't need the income.

In these situations the extra income may be appreciated, but there are two drawbacks. Firstly, you may be losing out on increasing that income in later years when you are totally dependent on it, and secondly that pension income is being added to the rest of your income and you will be liable to tax on your entire income including the pension.

Example
Rob White left his job and drew his pension of £15,000 a year at his firm's normal retirement age of 60. Prior to leaving work his salary was £30,000 a year and after tax and National Insurance he took home £1,885.30 a month. At 60 Rob felt he was too young to stop working and although he had come to dislike his job, mainly because of the politics of working for a large company, he actually enjoyed working. He was lucky enough to find another job that paid him £20,000 a year.

With his pension and new job he now took home £2,330.30 a month and decided he would like to save the difference for when he stops working altogether.

In this case Rob has a wide choice of saving options open to him but nearly all of them will involve him saving out of taxed income. However, if he saves the £445 a month extra income in a pension, tax relief will mean that his contribution will be increased to £556.25 a month.

Assuming 5% a year growth and charges of 1% a year, in five years time he would have a fund worth £36,993 compared with £28,955 from an investment that didn't have the same tax advantages. To be fair he can only take 25% of his fund as a tax-free lump sum and the rest has to be used to generate an income, but nonetheless it may be worth considering.

In order to receive tax relief on a pension you need to have earned income from working or self-employment (other types of income can also count but not income from a pension). Therefore this strategy is only worth considering if you are still working.

> **Insight**
>
> Once again I must stress the importance of separating
> the investment wrapper, in this case a pension, and the
> investment itself. Whenever I make a recommendation to
> a client for an arrangement such as this, I will nearly always
> recommend a conservative fund, sometimes even a deposit
> style arrangement and even then the minimum timescale will
> tend to be five years or more.

The second situation where a pension may be worth considering
at retirement is where you have a lump sum but need some extra
income. By investing the money in a pension and drawing tax
relief straightaway will mean that the amount you invest will
be increased as shown in the example below.

> **Example**
>
> Susan was about to retire and wanted to increase her income
> in such a way she could be sure that the income would never
> run out as long as she lived. She had £30,000 to invest and if
> she put that money in a pension the taxman would also put in
> an extra £7,500 in tax relief.

> **Insight**
>
> For this to work fully, Susan would have needed to have an
> earned income in the same tax year of at least £37,500 as the
> maximum tax relief cannot exceed your gross income.

ADVANTAGES OF A PENSION

The advantages of a pension can be summed up in one word: tax.
If you are a UK resident you will be able to claim tax relief on any
investment you place into a pension. Even if you don't pay any
Income Tax you can still put £3,600 a year into a pension and
obtain tax relief. The ability to obtain tax relief on contributions to
a pension is particularly attractive if you are a higher rate taxpayer
when you are making the contribution and a basic rate taxpayer
when you are drawing the benefit.

As well as tax relief on contributions, any growth in the fund is mainly free of tax.

DISADVANTAGES OF A PENSION

The main disadvantage of a pension is the limited way in which you can take benefits. You can take 25% of the value as a tax-free lump sum, and the rest needs to be taken as an income for the rest of your life.

The income from a pension is also taxable (but not subject to National Insurance) so the taxman does claw back some of the tax benefits you have been given.

WHERE TO GET ONE

Pensions are widely available and you can buy one directly from a provider such as an insurance company or through an intermediary such as an Independent Financial Adviser or a bank.

If you are investing in a pension for the reasons shown in the first example, i.e. you have an income that you don't need immediately, the usual key criteria is to find a provider that offers a conservative investment choice with a proven track record. Specifically what you are likely to need is what is known as a defensive managed fund *and* a cash or deposit fund.

Insight

The purpose of this strategy is to use the tax system to your advantage rather than an investment that may make a lot of money if it does well and lose a lot if it doesn't, which is why a very low-risk fund is so important. However, the amount you are considering investing in this way represents a small part of your overall wealth and if you want to take a more adventurous approach there is nothing to prevent you from doing so, but the choice must be yours.

If you are investing in order to draw an income from the pension immediately your requirement is different and what you need is the provider that will offer the best pension annuity rate. In this case the considerations are exactly the same as covered in Chapter 11.

Annuities

An annuity is an income that is purchased with a lump sum. An annuity bought outside of a pension is known as a Purchased Life Annuity (PLA) and the only difference is the tax treatment.

HOW DO THEY WORK?

With a Purchased Life Annuity (PLA) you pay a provider a lump sum and in return they will pay you an income for the rest of your life. The person who buys an annuity is known as an annuitant.

Theoretically you can also buy a non-pension annuity for a fixed period, say five or ten years, but in practice they are as rare as hen's teeth, and so to all intents and purposes can be ignored.

You may be able to secure a higher annuity income if you smoke, are in poor health or have a medical condition.

WHAT CHOICES ARE AVAILABLE?

The choices available under a Purchased Life Annuity are similar to those available for a pension annuity namely:

- *capital protection*
- *single or joint*
- *level or increasing*
- *payment frequency*
- *in advance or arrears*
- *with or without proportion.*

Capital protection
As the name suggests, capital protection protects your investment if you die within a certain period. Various options are available

including promising to return some of the lump sum if you die within a certain period. For example, a purchase price of £50,000 may buy you a Purchased Life Annuity that will pay an income of £2,500 a year for life with full capital protection. If you died after three years the difference between the capital paid and the income paid out will be returned, in this case £42,500.

Single or joint
A Purchased Life Annuity can be arranged on a single life basis where, unless capital protection has been included, they will stop on the death of the annuitant or on a joint life basis where payments will continue until the death of the second person.

Level or increasing
A PLA can be arranged so they pay the same amount of income for life or an increasing amount. The advantage of the former is the amount paid will be higher, the disadvantage is that over the years inflation will erode the value.

Payment frequency
You can usually choose to have the annuity paid annually, quarterly or monthly. Generally speaking the less frequently you have the income paid the greater the income, but usually only by a small amount.

In advance or in arrears
This refers to whether the amount is paid at the beginning of the payment period or the end. The first payment for an annual annuity paid in arrears will be made a year after the annuity has been purchased. Payments in arrears will tend to give a slightly higher income but the amount of increase will depend on the payment frequency. However, even annually in arrears will not make that much difference.

With or without proportion
This refers to whether or not the last payment will be made after you die. For example, if you select an annuity with proportion, it will make one final payment after you have died. An annuity without proportion will pay a slightly higher amount but not by much, especially for monthly payments.

HOW ARE THEY TAXED?

You will not receive tax relief on the money you invest into a Purchased Life Annuity. In respect of the income you receive, part of the money you receive is treated as a return of the capital you have invested and part interest payment. The split between capital and income is governed by HMRC tables based on average life expectancy for a person of a given age.

This split between capital and interest is purely for tax purposes and you will receive a single payment after the annuity provider has deducted basic rate tax on the interest proportion. If you are a non-taxpayer you can obtain a form from the annuity provider requesting that tax is not deducted. If you are a higher rate taxpayer you will be liable for the difference between basic rate and higher rate tax.

Insight
You can use the lump sum from a pension to buy a Purchased Life Annuity and because of the difference in tax treatment you may obtain a higher income by using that lump sum to buy a Purchased Life Annuity rather than taking all of your pension as income.

WHAT ARE THE CHARGES?

The charges for a Purchased Life Annuity are included as part of the rate paid.

WHAT ARE THE ADVANTAGES?

The advantages of a Purchased Life Annuity are:

▶ *You have an income for life that cannot run out.*
▶ *There is no investment risk.*
▶ *Depending on your age they may pay a higher income than other forms of secure investment.*

WHAT ARE THE DISADVANTAGES?

The disadvantages of a Purchased Life Annuity are:

- ▶ *You give up your capital.*
- ▶ *Once purchased you cannot change your mind.*
- ▶ *Economic conditions may change.*

This last point warrants further explanation. When you buy a Purchased Life Annuity the rate is set for the rest of your life. Even if you select an increasing annuity the amount that it will increase by will be agreed at outset. If economic conditions change over the years, for instance inflation could rise to a much higher level than existed when the annuity was set up, the value could quickly be eroded.

Insight

Purchased Life Annuities do have their advantages but it is fair to say they are not particularly popular, mainly because they involve handing over your capital forever. The older you are the better value they become simply because your life expectancy is less. They may appeal if you have a need for an income that cannot run out whilst you are still alive.

WHERE TO BUY ONE

A number of life assurance companies offer Purchased Life Annuities: the problem is finding which one is the best. Unlike pension annuities where tables are published showing the best rates, finding a table for Purchased Life Annuities is nigh on impossible. Even those that appear on internet search engines turn out to be the pension version.

This gives you two alternatives: either you can shop around insurance companies for yourself or contact an Independent Financial Adviser and ask them to search for you.

WHAT HAPPENS IF THINGS GO WRONG?

If your Purchased Life Annuity provider becomes insolvent, you will normally be protected by the Financial Services Compensation Scheme (FSCS) for 90% of the investment with no upper limit. Before you buy a Purchased Life Annuity you should be provided with a Key Features Document that will confirm if your provider is protected by the scheme. If the document doesn't explicitly say you will be covered then you would be strongly advised to find another provider who is.

THINGS TO WATCH OUT FOR

There aren't really any catches with a Purchased Life Annuity. You pay your lump sum and then receive your income. The main point is to shop around to find the best deal and think carefully before putting pen to paper as once you have signed to go ahead you will only have 30 days to change your mind and then you are committed to the contract for the rest of your life.

TEN POINTS TO REMEMBER

1 A pension can be worth considering as an investment when you retire if:
   ▷ You are working and drawing income from a pension and want to save some of this income.
   ▷ You have a lump sum to invest for income.

2 The advantage of both of these strategies is you can use the tax system to your advantage.

3 For the strategy to work you need income from working in the same tax year that you make the contribution.

4 If you are saving in a pension whilst still working you will usually want to invest in a conservative fund.

5 If you are investing in a pension to immediately draw an income, your requirement is to find the best pension annuity rates.

6 An annuity is an income payable for life that you buy with a lump sum (which can include your pension lump sum).

7 If you only want income from a defined contribution pension, due to the tax treatment you may be better off still taking your lump sum and investing in a Purchased Life Annuity.

8 There is a wide choice as to how an income from an annuity can be paid including being able to protect your capital if you die shortly after taking it out.

9 You may be able to secure a higher annuity income if you smoke, are in poor health or have a medical condition.

10 Finding the best rate for a Purchased Life Annuity can be difficult as comparison tables are not widely available, so it may be worth asking a financial adviser to shop around for you.

13

Ongoing investment strategy

In this chapter you will:
- *consider when you should review your savings and investments*
- *think about where to obtain information*
- *learn how to use that information*

Insight

Too many investors and their advisers make an investment decision and then forget about it, but like a car an investment needs regular maintenance. Deposit accounts can reduce their interest rates overnight from one that is extremely competitive to one that is not. More complex investments need reviewing on a regular basis to ensure that they are still achieving their original objective and in all cases a change in your circumstances could mean an investment is no longer suitable.

When should you review your savings and investments?

You should review your savings and investments on a regular basis and whenever your circumstances change including:

- ▶ *when you take benefits from a pension*
- ▶ *when you stop working, change your hours or job*
- ▶ *when your income changes for any reason.*

The reason for doing this is to make sure the investment is still suitable for your circumstances, including:

▶ *Is the investment producing growth when you need income?*
▶ *Does it still match your attitude to investment risk?*
▶ *Will you now need access to your money either immediately or in the foreseeable future?*

These aspects are explored a little further below.

IS THE INVESTMENT PRODUCING GROWTH WHEN YOU NEED INCOME?

You may have taken out savings or investment in order to build up a lump sum, but now you need to change that to produce an income. In an ideal world, even if you need an income it is best to have some growth as well, in order to protect you against inflation. However this is not always possible and you may have to compromise.

DOES IT STILL MATCH YOUR ATTITUDE TO INVESTMENT RISK?

This is perhaps the most important aspect of all. Changing circumstances can mean a change in how you feel about investment risk. When you were working you may have been prepared to take a higher risk because to a certain extent you replace any losses from income. This may no longer be so. On the other hand, you may take the view you need to take a higher risk in order to generate more income.

WILL I NEED ACCESS TO MY MONEY EITHER NOW OR IN THE FORESEEABLE FUTURE?

Changing circumstances may mean that you will need access to your money, when in the past this was not so important. You may need to draw on your savings and investments for any number of reasons; repairs to your home, a special holiday, the need to buy a new car are all examples of this. If your savings and investment are tied up in plans where you cannot get to them, or where the value could quickly fall, it is worth considering moving them to a more accessible alternative.

REGULAR REVIEWS

Even if your circumstances don't change you still need to review your savings and investments on a regular basis to make sure that they are still on track to achieve what you expected.

Insight

The advent of the internet has made reviewing savings and investments much easier, as many can now be instantly viewed online. Whilst this is undoubtedly a good thing, guard yourself against becoming too obsessed about short-term changes in your investment, either up or down. I feel checking once or twice a year is about right in this respect.

What should you review?

When reviewing your savings and investments there is a slightly different perspective for deposit accounts and investments such as OEICs and Unit Trusts.

DEPOSIT ACCOUNTS

For deposit accounts the primary requirement is to ensure that you are still getting the best rate of interest. Often banks and building societies will offer an attractive rate in order to attract new business only quietly to drop the rate a few months later.

Insight

The timing of when you check the rate you are receiving is important. Often the rate on offer will be higher in the

(Contd)

February to April period when many people are shopping around for the best rate, particularly for ISAs. Therefore a good time to check the rate you are receiving is June or December when most people's minds are on other things such as holidays and Christmas.

The other point is to make sure the rate you check is the rate you are receiving on your specific account. It is not unusual for there to be different series of accounts, for example, a series 3 cash ISA may pay less interest than a series 4.

UNIT TRUSTS/OEICs, INVESTMENT BONDS AND OTHER INVESTMENTS

For investments, rather than comparing rates on a certain day you will want to check how your investment has performed over time both against other similar investments and your expectations.

The second issue is relatively easy to deal with as when you originally made the investment you should have done so in the knowledge of what to expect in terms of rises and falls in value. Certainly if you made the investment on the basis of professional advice this should have been made crystal clear to you.

If the investment has fallen by more than you expected you may need to investigate further as there may be a good reason. In 2007–8 many cautious funds fell by 20–30% when you would usually only expect such a fund to fall between 10–15%. The reason for this exception was the extraordinary economic circumstances at the time.

Insight

The events of 2007–8 highlight an important point and that is not to be too concerned about a single set of results, provided of course there is a reason for it. Much of the losses of 2007–8 had largely recovered by the end of 2009.

As well as an investment falling, an investment rising by more than you expected is also cause for concern if it continues for more than a year or so. Large short-term rises, as happened in 2009, will happen from time to time, usually because they are recovering from large falls in the previous years. However if this continues much beyond a year or so alarm bells should start to ring.

Insight

Commercial property funds provided a perfect example of this. In the five years leading up to 2007 these funds had consistently produced returns way above the long-term average for such investments, with the average fund returning 18.3% in 2005 and 23.8% in 2006. This high level of growth was unsustainable and in the period from November 2007 to November 2008 the average property fund fell by 31%. The old adage of 'if it looks too good to be true, it probably is' is a good maxim to follow.

The second aspect of performance is how well the actual investment has performed when compared with other similar investments, but comparing like for like can be extremely difficult.

In a rising market an investment manager may appear to be underperforming against his or her peers because that manager has taken a more conservative stance that will pay dividends when the market falls. Alternatively they may be underperforming because they are not very good.

Nonetheless, if your particular investment has performed below the average for its sector for more than a year it is worth asking why.

When to sell out?

The other thing to consider when reviewing your investment, particularly if it is one that can fluctuate in value, is when you should take the gains you have made. There is no right or wrong answer to this and the decision will depend on a number of factors, the most important being:

▶ *how long you have held the investment for*
▶ *how long will it be before you think you will need to access it*
▶ *whether it is currently at a high point or a low point.*

All these factors need to be considered together. If you have held the investment for a long time, it is at a high point and you are getting towards the end of your investment timescale, then preserving what you have acquired to date becomes the most important factor. Providing there are no penalties for doing so it will make sense to move the money to a safer haven.

If, on the other hand, you are only one year into a ten-year intended time period, and the value has fallen, then the best advice is usually to stay put.

DIPS, PEAKS AND CRASHES

If you have a balanced investment portfolio or (put into English) not all your eggs are in one basket, you will have a degree of protection against falls and crashes.

Even after all the economic upheavals of 2007 and 2008, in November 2009 the average balanced Unit Trust/OEIC had returned 29.4% over five years and yet just one year earlier things would have seemed very much worse.

Insight

The key is to look at your returns over the entire period and not look at peaks and troughs in isolation. This is not easy to do, especially as human nature means we will tend to feel more aggrieved about a 10% fall in value in the last year than the 60% growth we have made in the previous five.

The important point when looking at the current value is to bear in mind the characteristics of the investment itself. You would expect a deposit account to steadily increase year by year (provided of course you haven't withdrawn more than the interest you have received). On the other hand, you would expect an investment in most OEICs to rise and fall in value.

Insight

This reiterates the point that you should understand the characteristics of an investment before you commit a single penny. If you knew that it may fall as well as rise in value then it should come as no surprise if in some years the value has fallen. In which case the issue is not so much whether or not it has fallen in value, but has it fallen more than you would have expected.

Where to find the information

DEPOSIT ACCOUNTS

For deposit accounts you will need to obtain the rate for your specific account and then compare that against others that are available. The best way of finding the rate for your existing account is to contact the provider and ask them.

To find the best rates available you could walk up and down the high street, but a far more effective way is to look in the newspaper or visit comparison websites. Most papers publish a list of best rates at least once a week.

If you use comparison websites you need to be aware that they charge the organizations that are listed a fee, so you can't always be sure the very best will be listed.

The other thing is to make sure you compare like for like as terms and conditions vary between accounts.

For investments you need to make sure you compare how your investment has performed over exactly the same timescale as those you are comparing with as even a few weeks difference can distort things considerably. There are a number of websites that list most funds in the UK (see the back of the book for more details).

Theory and practice

In theory, reviewing and comparing your savings and investments should be easy. You just look at how well they are performing and compare them with others that are similar.

In practice it is not that easy, as there are so many different permutations and differences that can explain differences in performance. These variations are impossible to cover in a book such as this, or perhaps any book as experience is an important factor in making the judgement calls that are required to stick with an investment or move on to another.

This means that you may want an adviser to do this for you, particularly if they set the investment up for you in the first place.

TEN POINTS TO REMEMBER

1 You should review your savings and investments on a regular basis, at least once a year.

2 You should also review if your circumstances change to make sure they are still suitable for you.

3 Avoid comparing deposit rates in February–April when rates can be artificially high to attract business.

4 For investments such as Unit Trusts you need to check:
   ▷ if the investment is performing in line with your expectations
   ▷ how the investment is performing against its peers.

5 Do not be concerned about short-term changes, longer-term trends are more important.

6 Be as wary of increases over and above your expectations as falls in value.

7 If you are nearing the end of your investment timescale and your investment has done well, it can be worth selling out early, providing there aren't penalties for doing so.

8 Try not to panic about falls in value shortly after taking out an investment. Selling out in this situation can just mean turning a paper loss into a real one.

9 When making comparisons make sure you identify your actual investment and compare like for like.

10 Because of the numerous points to consider it may be worth using an adviser to review your investments for you.

14

Equity release

In this chapter you will:
- **consider when equity release might be appropriate for you**
- **learn where to find advice on equity release plans**
- **find out about Home Reversion Plans and Lifetime Mortgages**

Equity release is a way of releasing some or all of the capital that has built up in your home to generate a lump sum or income. It is true to say that this area of retirement planning has had a shocking reputation, some of which is entirely justified and as a result many will not even consider this method of improving their standard of living.

This is a shame because in the right circumstances it can be an effective way of raising capital and/or increasing income, especially in the later years of retirement. The industry is now regulated and there has been a massive improvement in standards over the years.

Insight
For reasons that will be explained in this chapter, equity release will rarely be suitable for someone who has only just retired. However whether or not you would be prepared to sell or remortgage part of your home later in retirement is something you should consider when first retiring as it can influence the decisions you make at that time.

How does equity release work?

Equity release is a way of releasing capital from your home whilst continuing to live in it. This is achieved in one of two ways:

- ▶ *selling part of your home – known as Home Reversion Plans*
- ▶ *remortgaging part of your home – known as lifetime mortgages.*

In both instances you retain the right to continue living in your home until you die or permanently enter nursing care.

Insight

Equity release should not be confused with lease-back schemes where you sell your home and then rent it back. With equity release you do not pay rent and you cannot be thrown out of your home. Furthermore, all reputable equity release schemes have a guarantee that means your relatives won't be left with a debt when you die.

Why does equity release have such a bad reputation?

Before going any further it is worth discussing why equity release has such a bad reputation. The main reason for this is that when equity release products were originally put on the market, the way they worked meant you could actually be worse off after you had taken one out than before.

There were a number of reasons for this. One was that many had variable interest rates that were payable on the loan, but they only generated a fixed income. If the interest payments rose above the income then you could find yourself paying out more than you received.

Others were directly linked to investment products and if the investment underperformed you could be worse off. In extreme cases some customers had to pay more in interest than they received in income *and* their estates were left owing money to the provider after the customer had died.

Also, neither the product or the sales process were regulated which meant that unsuitable products were inappropriately sold. This was not the case across the board but it happened enough to give the product a reputation that lingers to this day.

However, that reputation does not reflect modern practices. These days the following exist to protect you:

▶ *Advice on equity release is regulated by the FSA.*
▶ *There is usually a 'no negative equity' guarantee.*
▶ *For Lifetime Mortgages there is no repayment of interest or capital until death or entering nursing care.*

Advice regulated by the FSA
The FSA is the organization that oversees the advice given on financial products sold in the UK. Equity release is one of those areas where you should obtain advice before proceeding. The FSA's rules require that the adviser must ensure that the product is suitable for you and that you understand all the disadvantages as well as the benefits. Advisers have to be specifically authorized and qualified to give advice on equity release.

'No negative equity' guarantee
Most equity release products have a 'no negative equity' guarantee. This means you can never owe more than the value of your home. If an equity release product doesn't have this guarantee then walk away.

For Lifetime Mortgages there is no repayment of interest or capital until death or entering nursing care
Instead of paying interest on a monthly basis, all of the interest is repaid when you die or permanently move into long-term care.

This means you can never pay out more then you receive in income.

> ## Insight
>
> As well as being regulated by the FSA, all reputable equity release providers belong to an organization known as SHIP which stands for Safe Home Income Plans. SHIP sets out a minimum set of standards for these products, including the 'no negative equity' guarantee. You should only ever consider an equity release product from a SHIP member.

Types of equity release plans

There are two types of equity release plan:

▶ *Home Reversion Plans*
▶ *Lifetime Mortgages*

HOME REVERSION PLANS

With a Home Reversion Plan you sell all or part of your home to a provider in return for a cash sum. (In Scotland the maximum that can be sold is 99%.) You then have the right to continue living in your home rent-free until you die or move permanently into long-term care.

If you own your home with another person then the plan runs until the last person dies or moves permanently into long-term care.

If you sell all of your home, then the Home Reversion Plan provider will benefit from all of the increase in the value of your property. If you only sell part then you and the provider will benefit from the increases in line with the proportion that you own.

> ### Example
>
> Peter Jackson was 70 when he took out a Home Reversion Plan. He sold 30% of his house which at that time was worth £250,000, giving him a lump sum of £75,000.
>
> By the time he died at age 87 his house was worth £375,000 so Peter's estate would be entitled to £262,500 (70% of £375,000) and the HRP provider would be entitled to £112,500 (30% of £375,000).

LIFETIME MORTGAGES

Unlike a Home Reversion Plan, with a Lifetime Mortgage you retain full ownership of your home. The money is raised by you taking out a mortgage on it.

Unlike other mortgages, there is no fixed period on the loan which is repaid on your death (second death in the case of a couple), or you permanently move into long-term care (second person in the case of a couple).

You do not pay the interest immediately. Instead it is 'rolled up' to be repaid when the capital is repaid.

> ### Example
>
> Jackie Smith was aged 70 and her house was worth £250,000 when she took out an equity release plan that provided her with a cash sum of £75,000.
>
> By the time she died at age 87 her house was worth £375,000, the entire value of which passed to her estate which was liable to repay the loan capital and interest of £112,500 from the estate.

There are three types of Lifetime Mortgage:

▶ *Capital Release Plans*
▶ *Income Plans*
▶ *Drawdown Plans*

Capital Release Plans

A Capital Release Plan allows you to release a single lump sum to spend as you wish. Because the amount received is capital, there is no Income Tax or Capital Gains Tax payable, although if the money is invested then Income Tax or CGT may be payable on the income or growth.

In contrast to the other types of Lifetime Mortgages, the capital is taken as a single amount.

> ### *Example*
> Maggie Jackson is 73 and has a home worth £175,000. She takes out a Capital Release Plan for £68,250 which is paid to her as a single lump sum. When she dies or goes into long-term care all of the £68,250 plus interest must be paid to the provider.

Income Plans

Whilst some income plans create an annuity, in the vast majority of cases the term income is a misnomer as the amounts paid are actually instalments of capital.

With these plans the total amount of the loan is agreed at outset and this is then released in instalments over an agreed number of years. The interest rate is also agreed at outset and will remain the same for the entire period of the mortgage.

Because the 'income' is actually instalments of capital, no Income Tax is payable.

> ### *Example*
> Reg King is aged 67 and needs income. His house is worth £270,000 and he can borrow a maximum of £72,900. This will be paid out to him at monthly intervals for the next ten years, giving him a monthly income of £607.50.

He only pays interest on the amount of the mortgage that has actually been paid out so if he dies after five years only the amount paid out, i.e. £36,450, and the interest on that capital will need to be repaid.

Drawdown Plans

With a Drawdown Plan you are given a total amount that you can borrow over a period of time and you can access those funds as and when you need them.

The total amount of the loan that will be available is known as the maximum loan. Usually you will take an amount at outset (known as the starting loan) and the difference between the starting loan and the total maximum loan is known as the reserve. You can then draw on this reserve (subject to certain conditions) within a certain time period, for example 15 years.

Example

Margaret and John Blake have a house worth £250,000. They are able to secure a lifetime mortgage with a total maximum loan of £75,000. Of this they need to access £25,000 immediately to buy a new car and support their income for the next three years.

This leaves £50,000 that they can access at any time in the next 15 years, subject to a minimum withdrawal of £2,000.

ADVANTAGES OF HOME REVERSION PLANS OVER LIFETIME MORTGAGES

The main advantages of Home Reversion Plans over Lifetime Mortgages are:

▶ *It will usually be possible to release more equity with a Home Reversion Plan, with the possibility to sell up to 100% (99% in Scotland) to release equity irrespective of age. The usual maximum that can be released with a Lifetime Mortgage is between 20–50%, depending on the age of the borrower.*
▶ *If interest rates are high and house inflation is low, then a Home Reversion Plan may represent better value, although this will depend on the precise circumstances.*

ADVANTAGES OF LIFETIME MORTGAGES
OVER HOME REVERSION PLANS

The main advantages of Lifetime Mortgages over Home Reversion Plans are:

▶ *The borrower retains full ownership of their home. Apart from the emotional reassurance this may bring, it makes it slightly easier to reverse the decision to release equity by paying off all or part of the loan if circumstances change, for example through an inheritance.*
▶ *If interest rates are low and house inflation is high then a Lifetime Mortgage may represent better value as the increase in the house value will outstrip the interest roll-up.*

When should you consider equity release?

As well as considering equity release when you might actually need additional income or capital, you should also think about whether you may consider it at a later stage when you first retire.

If you are prepared to consider equity release at a later stage, then it can influence some of the decisions you have to make when you first retire including:

▶ *whether you are prepared to take a pension that starts higher but doesn't increase with inflation*
▶ *whether you will use drawdown rather than buy an annuity in the knowledge that if your capital erodes as a result then you can replace it with equity from your home*
▶ *whether you are prepared to release equity from your home at a later stage – if this is the case then you may be prepared to take a slightly more adventurous approach to your investments.*

Insight

Unless you have no alternative, in my opinion equity release doesn't start to look an attractive proposition until you are at least age 70 and more often 75. This is because any younger and the impact on the mortgage roll-up, or potential for missing out on any property increase is simply too high. For example, a lifetime mortgage of £50,000 with an interest rate of 6% would mean that over 15 years the interest would add up to £48,996; over 25 years that interest would total £111,255.

THINGS TO CONSIDER BEFORE ENTERING INTO EQUITY RELEASE

Whilst most Home Reversion Plans allow you to buy back the proportion of your home that you have sold, and nearly all Lifetime Mortgages will allow you to repay the loan, in practice once you have taken out an equity release plan it will be very difficult to reverse the decision. This means that you need to think very carefully before proceeding and take the following into account:

▶ *what alternatives are available*
▶ *the impact on state benefits*
▶ *it will reduce any legacy you wish to leave.*

What alternatives are available?

Many advisers consider that equity release should be the very last thing you should consider in order to raise capital or increase your income, simply because once made the decision will almost certainly stay with you for the rest of your life.

Therefore you should explore all the alternatives, including whether you would be better off trading down, whether you could be eligible for state benefits or you could raise the money in some other way. If you use an adviser they should do this for you.

The impact on state benefits

Whilst the value of your home is taken into account for some state benefits, this is not always the case, and using equity release may prevent you from claiming some of these benefits. Therefore you should investigate this and once again an adviser should do this for you as part of their recommendation.

It will reduce any legacy you wish to leave

Many people wish to leave their children and grandchildren a sum of money when they die. Often this will include the value of their home. If you release capital from your home then this will be reduced.

Insight

I tend to find that whilst the person considering equity release is concerned about this point, the children who will benefit are not, often preferring their parents to have an improved standard of living whilst they are alive rather than benefit someone else when they are dead. Either way it is often a good idea to discuss this with your family before going ahead.

Finding a provider

Whilst you can take out an equity release plan directly with a provider, this is an area where you should seek independent advice. This is not only due to the complexities but also you have a 'come back' if something goes wrong. In fact some equity release providers will only deal through an adviser so you may not be able to get the best deal directly.

The adviser should be regulated by the FSA, and have the additional authorization required to deal with this type of business. You should ask them to provide evidence of their experience in this area.

The adviser should spend at least as much time pointing out why you shouldn't go ahead, as selling you the benefits.

You should also consider paying a fee to obtain a report on the pros and cons on whether or not you should proceed.

TEN POINTS TO REMEMBER

1 *Consider equity release when you first retire as well as when you actually might need it.*

2 *The poor reputation equity release suffers from is largely due to the way the product was structured and sold in the past. Since then many improvements mean this reputation is unwarranted.*

3 *Only ever take out an equity release plan with a Safe Home Income Plans (SHIP) provider as they have a number of conditions to make the process a lot safer including a 'no negative equity' guarantee.*

4 *An adviser has to be specifically authorized by the FSA in order to advise on equity release. Always obtain proof that they are.*

5 *There are two types of plan, Home Reversion Plan and Lifetime Mortgage.*

6 *With a Home Reversion Plan you sell all or part of your home to the provider but retain the right to live there for life or until the last plan holder permanently enters long-term care.*

7 *With a Lifetime Mortgage you retain ownership but take out a mortgage where the interest and capital is repaid on death or until the last plan holder permanently enters long-term care.*

8 *There are three types of Lifetime Mortgage:*
  ▷ *Capital Release Plans*
  ▷ *Income Plans*
  ▷ *Drawdown Plans*

9 *Before entering into equity release you should always investigate the alternatives such as trading down to a cheaper property.*

10 *You need to understand the impact equity release could have on state benefits and any legacy you may wish to leave when you die.*

15

....

Getting advice

In this chapter you will learn:

- *about the different types of financial adviser and where to find one*
- *about how to get the most from an adviser*
- *about the process an adviser should follow and the documents they should provide you with*

Insight

The object of this book is to help you prepare and make the most of your finances in the run-up to and following retirement. However, I would be first to admit that, whilst the basics are sometimes straightforward, the detail can be highly complex. Also it is impossible in a book such as this to cover the multitude of different issues, circumstances and exceptions that will apply to you as an individual. Because of this you may decide to seek professional advice.

Hopefully reading this book will go a long way to help you understand the issues involved in planning financially for retirement, but you may also want to seek additional personal advice, for example, help in finding the most suitable provider for your particular circumstances.

This book should help you know what to ask and look out for. Knowing where to turn to obtain sound, trustworthy financial advice can be extremely difficult at any stage in life and retirement planning is no different.

This chapter will cover how to find an adviser and how to make the most of their services including:

▶ *what types of advisers are available and the differences between them*
▶ *where to find an adviser*
▶ *what you should know about financial advisers*
▶ *how to get the most from a financial adviser*
▶ *the process you should expect an adviser to follow*
▶ *the documents they should provide you with.*

It will also outline other sources of support and information:

▶ *your employer*
▶ *citizens' advice*
▶ *government agencies.*

What types of adviser are there?

The rules governing most financial advice in the UK are set by the Financial Services Authority (FSA) and until relatively recently there were only two types of adviser:

▶ *an independent adviser who acted for you and was not tied to a particular provider*
▶ *a tied adviser who could only advise on one company's products.*

This has now changed and currently there are three types of adviser:

▶ *independent*
▶ *whole-of-market*
▶ *tied.*

Insight

Proposals are in place that may see this change but, irrespective of the FSA's rules, advisers are likely to always fall into one or more of the following camps:

- ▶ *Financial advisers who act for you as opposed to those who act for the companies whose products they sell.*
- ▶ *Advisers who deal with one or a limited number of companies.*
- ▶ *Advisers who search the entire market on your behalf to find the most suitable product for you.*

Some advisers will charge you a fee, others will obtain commission from a product provider, and others offer a mixture of both.

INDEPENDENT ADVISERS

An Independent Financial Adviser (IFA) acts for you and is required by the FSA to find the most suitable product and provider for your specific circumstances. If they arrange an investment product, including a pension, they must give you the opportunity to pay by a fee rather than receiving commission from the product provider.

Often they will give you a choice of whether you want to pay a fee or whether you would prefer them to be paid by commission, or a mixture of both. Some IFAs will only work on a fee basis and nearly all will charge a fee if the advice they provide doesn't involve them arranging a product for you.

If you decide on a fee, then any commission the IFA receives has to be refunded to you although this will usually be done by enhancing the product benefits or reducing the product charges as this tends to be more tax efficient for you and them.

The fee can be expressed in a number of ways, for example it can be an hourly rate, a fixed fee for the work carried out, or a percentage of any investment you make.

However they are paid, an IFA is obliged to explain what and how they charge you before carrying out any work on your behalf.

WHOLE-OF-MARKET

A whole-of-market adviser is similar to an IFA in that they have access to the whole of the market, but legally they act for the provider rather than for you and usually will only work on a commission basis.

TIED

As far as the regulation is concerned there is only one type of tied adviser, but in practice they can be subdivided into single-tied or multi-tied.

A single-tied adviser can only sell one company's products. Perhaps the most famous example of this type of adviser was the traditional 'insurance man' who called at regular intervals.

A multi-tied adviser deals with more than one company. The number of companies varies, although in practice the range tends to be limited. The advantage of this type of adviser over a single-tied adviser is that they are more likely to have access to a product that is particularly suited to your individual circumstances but this cannot be guaranteed.

Whether an adviser is single-tied or multi-tied, legally they do not act for you, they are acting for the company's or companies' products that they are selling and they will nearly always be paid by commission.

Many banks and building societies now operate on this basis.

What you should know about financial advisers

Whilst there are many thousands of honest and highly skilled financial advisers in the UK there are a few things you need to understand about how the financial services industry has worked in the past and to a large extent still works today. These points are:

▶ *the way financial advisers are paid*
▶ *the level of qualification required to be a financial adviser.*

THE WAY FINANCIAL ADVISERS ARE PAID

In the past, the vast majority of financial advisers have been paid by receiving commission on the products that they sell or arrange. Whilst there are some advantages to this, most notably you don't have to pay out a separate fee, there are some issues.

Firstly the adviser only gets paid if a product is sold. Whilst there are thousands of honest advisers who did and still do give excellent advice under this system it can create problems including:

▶ *Sometimes you will need advice that is not linked to a product in any way. If the adviser only gets paid for arranging a product then there may be a temptation to advise you to take out a product that may not be needed.*
▶ *You may be sold the product that earns the most commission rather than the one that is best for you.*
▶ *You may find that the adviser is unwilling to help you if there is little possibility of them earning anything from the transaction. After all they have to make a living too!*

Whilst the situation is changing, and more and more advisers are charging fees, you need to be aware that the vast majority of advisers still need to earn commission in order to survive. Even in the case where the advisers themselves don't earn commission, their firm probably will.

There are some circumstances where the adviser earning commission will genuinely mean the advice to you is free, but these are very rare indeed. In the vast majority of situations when the adviser takes commission, you will be paying through the product charges.

This is not necessarily a bad thing. It can represent good value and a high level of convenience, but you need to know how much commission is costing you. The answer will very rarely be nothing – be very suspicious if that is what you are told.

The easy way to check how much commission is actually costing you is to ask your adviser to provide two quotes for any product they are recommending: one showing them taking no commission and one taking the level of commission they will be charging you. This way you can see the true cost of the commission.

Most independent advisers will be happy to do this for you as they must give you the opportunity to pay a fee rather than take commission for most products that they deal with. If a whole-of-market or tied adviser is unwilling or unable to do this for you then you may be better off shopping around for an alternative source of advice.

Insight

As an IFA, I sometimes find it difficult to explain to prospective clients that they have to pay me a fee when they can obtain 'free' advice elsewhere, but increasingly more and more people are realizing that, as is so often the case, few things are rarely genuinely free.

THE LEVEL OF KNOWLEDGE

Historically, most financial advisers were recruited on their ability to sell rather than their ability to advise. Over the years this has changed enormously, with the regulator imposing minimum standards and every adviser now has to be competent to carry out the role.

However, the basic threshold is much lower than for professions such as accountants or lawyers. This is not to say that experience can't take the place of formal qualifications, and just because someone can pass an exam doesn't mean to say they make a good adviser.

Unfortunately when it comes to qualifications there is a rather an 'alphabet soup' of initials advisers can put after their name. The table below outlines most of the main qualifications.

Level	Qualification	Designatory Letters
Basic minimum requirement	Financial Planning Certificate	Cert PFS
	Certificate in Financial Planning	Cert PFS
	Certificate for Financial Advisors	CeFA
Advanced level	Advanced Financial Planning Certificate	DipFPS
	Diploma in Financial Planning	DipFPS
	Diploma for Financial Advisers	DipFA
More advanced	Advanced Diploma in Financial Planning	APFS
Top	Chartered Financial Planner	CFP
	Certified Financial Planner	CFP

As well as the pieces of paper it is important to check the adviser has the experience to deal with your particular circumstances, as even Chartered or Certified Planners cannot be experts in everything (in fact be extremely wary of anyone who indicates that they are!).

The only way to check this is to ask the adviser what experience they have of dealing with your particular issue and ask to see examples of reports they have written to other customers or names of existing customers you can refer to for a reference.

Selecting an adviser

Selecting an adviser is not easy, not least because you can't physically see the product or service that they are providing. Also it may be many years before you know if you have received good or bad advice.

Although there some large IFA firms, most tend to be relatively small businesses run locally. This means that you cannot be guided by a big name brand that you can trust.

On the other hand, most big names that you recognize, such as banks and building societies, will tend to be tied advisers of one sort or another.

To make matters worse it can sometimes be difficult to tell the difference between an IFA, whole-of-market and tied adviser. Even though the FSA maintain a register of advisers so you can check if the person who is providing you with advice is authorized or not, it says nothing about whether the person or their firm is independent or tied.

Finding a financial adviser will largely depend on what type of adviser you require. If you are happy with tied advice, then nearly every bank and building society will be able to advise you on this basis, and all you need to do is contact your local branch.

You can find a lot of financial advisers via the internet, but as usual separating the wheat from the chaff can be extremely difficult. For example, if you type 'Financial Adviser' into a search engine you will get literally millions of entries from specialist search engines to individual firms. Even if you type in 'Independent Financial Adviser', a lot of the companies that are listed are not independent at all.

Before you despair and think that finding a good financial adviser is impossible, the following should help.

HOW TO FIND A FINANCIAL ADVISER THAT WILL MEET YOUR REQUIREMENTS

You will stand the greatest chance of finding an adviser who will best serve your needs if you take the following steps:

▶ *Separate the issue of receiving advice and buying a product.*
▶ *Be prepared to pay a fee for the advice.*
▶ *Use an Independent Financial Adviser.*
▶ *Expect the adviser to be totally open from the very beginning about the way and how much they are paid.*
▶ *Check the level of qualification and experience.*
▶ *Expect the adviser to spend time finding out about you and your requirements.*
▶ *Make sure you understand what is being suggested.*
▶ *Expect the adviser to point out the downsides of any course of action as well as the benefits.*

Separate the issue of receiving advice and buying a product

Usually receiving advice and buying a financial service product are wrapped into the same process. However, they are in fact separate and more often than not the advice is more important and valuable than the actual product.

Insight

When you initially meet with a financial adviser, make it perfectly clear that you want advice on your requirements. Only when you have received that advice will you consider arranging a product if that is what has been suggested.

Be prepared to pay a fee

Following on from the point above, in order to ensure you receive unbiased advice rather than advice that leads to you buying a product, you need to be prepared to pay for that advice even if you agree to the adviser taking commission from any product they may go on and arrange for you.

It may be possible to come to an arrangement with the adviser whereby that if you subsequently ask them to arrange a product, any commission that they receive will be offset against the fee.

Expect the adviser to be totally open from the very beginning about what way and how much they are paid

Irrespective of what way they get paid, expect the adviser to be totally open from the outset about how much they will be paid. Most advisers for most classes of business now have to tell you how much they get paid for advising you, and what form that payment takes even if they get paid commission.

Insight

Even when they do not have to tell you how much they get paid, a reputable adviser will always be willing to give you this information. Be wary of anyone who says their advice is free.

Use an Independent Financial Adviser

The point of dealing with an IFA is twofold. Firstly, legally they act for you. This means that they have a responsibility to put your interests first. Secondly they have the ability to obtain products from the vast range of different companies and products that are available and so they should be able to find the most suitable product for you.

This ability to select from the whole of the market could mean there is a risk that the adviser will be tempted to recommend the product that pays them the highest commission rather than the one that is right for you. In practice this is less commonplace than you might imagine and the comments made earlier regarding commission will help you spot if this is happening.

Sometimes it can be difficult to tell if an adviser is actually independent or not and you need to be aware of statements such as 'independently owned'. Even checking the register of advisers maintained by the FSA will not provide you with this information.

The easiest way of finding an IFA is via the website (www.unbiased.co.uk). Unlike some other websites you can only be listed on Unbiased if you are an IFA. By entering your postcode and requirements you will be able to locate an IFA near to you.

Not all IFAs are listed on Unbiased, but all advisers whether independent or not have to provide you with a document that tells you if they are or not.

Insight

At this point I must admit to a bias as I am an IFA, but this is because I genuinely believe it is the only way to make sure I can give truly impartial advice and, where a client requires a product, find the best one for them.

Check the level of qualification and experience

Don't just rely on what the adviser tells you about their qualifications and experience. If a qualification is claimed then the adviser should have a certificate to prove it.

If you know someone who has dealt with the adviser, ask them their opinion. If you don't know anyone who has dealt with the adviser, or even if you do, ask the adviser for details of their actual experience in dealing with situations similar to yours, and perhaps ask to see samples of any reports they may have prepared for other customers.

Insight

We have examples of the various types of retirement reports that we prepare for clients, so any prospective or existing client can 'see before they buy'.

Expect the adviser to spend time finding out about you and your requirements

Immediately walk away from an adviser who tries to recommend a product or solution before spending time finding out what your requirements actually are.

In order to advise you effectively, an adviser should first spend time finding out what your requirements actually are. This can be a time-consuming process as to be done effectively a lot of detail is required, not only about your current circumstances but also about what you want to achieve.

Make sure you understand what is being suggested

It is often thought that the most important issue when finding a financial adviser is to find one you can trust. Whilst this is undoubtedly important it is at least as important to understand what is being recommended. Simply trusting your adviser to look after you could lead to unexpected results if only because you and they had different expectations.

Whilst you don't necessarily need to know all the detail of what happens 'under the bonnet', you do need to have a clear understanding of what could happen if the wheels come off.

Insight

One of the FSA's requirements of a financial adviser is that the adviser ensures that a client understands what is being recommended before proceeding. However you also have a responsibility in this area, after all it is your money, so it is worth taking the time to ensure you understand the cons as well as the pros of what is being recommended.

Expect the adviser to point out the downsides of any course of action as well as the benefits

There is no such thing as a perfect solution when it comes to financial advice and there is always a downside. For example, a very safe investment may not produce the income you need, whereas one that does give you the required level of income may pose a risk to your capital.

Some of the decisions you make when you retire will remain with you for the rest of your life and those decisions can be difficult and sometimes impossible to reverse, so it is vitally important to understand the cons as well as the pros. Therefore expect the adviser to spend some time with you explaining the disadvantages of what he or she is suggesting as well as the advantages.

Insight

In fact, in some areas such as equity release or the transfer of a defined benefit pension, it should almost seem as if the adviser is trying to talk you out of going ahead. In all cases they should clearly point out any disadvantages or risks involved.

The financial advice process

Whatever type of adviser you deal with, the process should be very similar as described below.

▶ *The adviser should explain what sort of adviser they are, how they work and how they get paid.*
▶ *The adviser should then spend some time finding out about you and your requirements.*
▶ *The adviser may need to obtain information on your existing arrangements.*
▶ *They will then spend some time preparing a recommendation.*
▶ *They will then present those recommendations to you.*
▶ *If any action is needed and you agree they will help you implement that action.*
▶ *They will confirm in writing what they have recommended and why.*

The adviser should explain what sort of adviser they are, how they work and how they get paid

The first time you deal with an adviser they should provide you with a written statement explaining how they do business. Often they will use a document known as a Services and Costs Disclosure Document (SCDD). Whether or not they use this actual document, they are required by the FSA to provide you with certain information about how they work and what they charge.

How well they explain this information is a good early indicator of how much time and trouble they will take in ensuring the advice you receive will be right for you. Ideally, instead of just giving you a piece of paper, the adviser should run through the document explaining what it actually means.

The adviser should spend some time finding out about you and your requirements

Once the adviser has told you about how they work, they should spend time finding out about your requirements. In practice many advisers will spend a little time doing this before they do anything else, but the bulk of the fact-finding process will usually take place after explaining how they work.

Even if you only require advice in one specific area, they will almost certainly run through a checklist of other areas where you may require financial advice. Whilst it may appear that they are simply doing this in order to try to sell you something else, there are in fact several valid reasons why they do this.

Firstly there may be some things that haven't occurred to you that may be worth considering as a higher priority than the area that you have initially asked for advice on. For example, you want advice about investments but looking at your pension at the same time could be relevant to the investment advice.

Secondly, in this litigious day and age, there is a fear that if an adviser doesn't at least flag other areas of potential need they may be held liable if it is consequently found (or even claimed) that those other areas should have taken a higher priority.

The adviser may need to obtain information on your existing arrangements

Once the adviser has found out what your requirements are, they may need to find out some information on your existing arrangements. There are a number of reasons for this, including advising you what they are worth and how suitable they are for your needs.

Usually this will involve contacting your existing provider for the required information and the adviser will ask for your written permission to do this.

Be prepared for this to take a little while. The standard response from many providers for any request for information is 'ten working days', and often it can take longer than that. It is also not unusual for the information supplied to be incomplete in some way meaning the adviser has to ask for it again.

During this process your adviser should keep you up to date with progress.

Insight

It can really be quite embarrassing sometimes how long it can take to gather all of the information required in order to advise a client, so it is best to approach an adviser at least two or three months before you intend to retire.

THEY WILL THEN SPEND SOME TIME PREPARING A RECOMMENDATION

Once the adviser has collated all the information, they will often need to carry out some research, such as assessing how well your existing plans have performed against other similar investments.

Even if they do not need to carry out research into your existing arrangements, they will almost certainly need to perform a number of calculations and obtain illustrations to make a recommendation to you.

They will then present those recommendations to you

They will then usually present the recommendations to you. This may be in the form of a written report, a verbal briefing or both.

At this stage make sure you fully understand what is being suggested and don't be pushed into making an instant decision if you want time to think about things. Remember you have engaged this person to advise you, not sell you something. If the suggestion is to replace an existing product with another one, ensure the reasons, benefits and disadvantages of doing so are fully explained.

If the recommendations include the suggestion for you to take out a product, the adviser will complete the paperwork in order to put this product in place.

Most products will have a cooling-off period and the product provider will write to you directly giving you a certain period to change your mind. If you no longer want to go ahead you will need to send the form back directly to the product provider not the adviser who arranged the product for you. If you want to go ahead you do not need to do anything.

They will confirm in writing what they have recommended and why

Finally, if the adviser has arranged a product they will usually have to confirm in writing why they consider the product they have arranged is suitable for you.

If they have already provided a written report as part of their recommendations, and you have acted on those recommendations, this may simply be a short letter confirming that the actions suggested have been carried out.

If you have not been provided with a written report already, for most products they must provide you with a Suitability Report outlining their understanding of your requirements and what they have recommended for you and why they have made that recommendation. If the recommendation included cancelling an existing arrangement, the report should explain why this has been suggested.

Ongoing 'maintenance'

As well as advising you initially, you may require ongoing advice, for example you may want to review your investments on an ongoing basis. If you want an ongoing service then you should discuss this with your adviser and find out how much it will cost.

Insight

Sometimes there is no need for an ongoing service. For example, in my firm, where a client's only requirement was to find the best pension annuity rate then there is not really an ongoing need and the fee we charge initially is the only fee the client has to pay. Where there is an ongoing requirement, for example to monitor investments, we provide our clients with several choices about the level of the service they require and the costs of providing that service.

Regulatory documents

When you buy a financial product you can't see what you are buying in the same way you can when you buy a physical item like a car or a TV. This means you are often totally dependent on what the adviser tells you about it.

One of the impacts of regulation has been to introduce documents that are designed to explain:

- ▶ *the nature of the relationship between you and the adviser or sales person*
- ▶ *how the product being recommended works*
- ▶ *why the adviser considers the product right for you.*

The documents that cover this are:

- ▶ *When you first start dealing with an adviser they should provide you with a Services and Costs Disclosure Document (SCDD) that sets out what services they will provide, how they will provide them and the costs of doing so.*
- ▶ *Before setting up any product you should be provided with a Key Features Document (KFD) that explains the product.*
- ▶ *Shortly after taking out the product you should be provided with a Suitability Report that explains why the adviser*

considers the product they are recommending is suitable for your needs.

Whilst these documents are intended to clarify the process, sometimes they can have the opposite effect. This can be due to the complexity of the disclosures or just simply the volume of paper you will be provided with. The key points to look for in each of these documents are:

Services and Costs Disclosure Document
This should tell you:

- ▶ *what type of adviser you are dealing with, e.g. tied or independent. If they are tied they should also provide you with a list of the companies they deal with.*
- ▶ *whether or not they will actually advise you or arrange products on your behalf. Believe it or not some advisers will not actually advise you, they will simply provide you with certain information and then leave you to decide if what is being suggested is suitable for you. In practice the dividing line between providing you with advice and simply giving you the facts can be very narrow, so please check this point carefully. Whilst the difference may seem academic, if you are given advice the adviser takes responsibility for that advice; if you are only provided with the facts and left to make your own decision you take the responsibility.*
- ▶ *how much you will have to pay for their services.*
- ▶ *who to complain to if something goes wrong.*

Key Features Document and Illustration
Depending on the product and provider these may be two separate documents or contained within a single document.

The Key Features Document (KFD) is intended to set out the main points of the contract that is being recommended. The trouble is that sometimes it is so long and detailed it only serves to confuse so this section will highlight the main sections that you really should read.

The object of the Illustration is to set out what you might get back if you go ahead and take out the product.

Insight

It is important to understand the purpose of an Illustration which is not the obvious one of showing you what your returns will be. The object of an Illustration is to show the impact of the product charges at the growth rates shown on the Illustration. It is not to show what you will get back as there is no guarantee that the returns will match those on the Illustration. The idea behind this is that you compare the charges between different products and providers.

You should always carefully check and make sure you understand the following sections of the KFD:

▶ *the aim of the plan*
▶ *what risks are involved*
▶ *your commitment.*

Whilst KFDs differ they will also usually cover the points listed below and, once again, reading and understanding them will go a long way to making sure you know what you are buying. The KFD should tell you:

▶ *where your money is invested*
▶ *the tax treatment of the plan*
▶ *the terms of any penalties for accessing your money within a certain time period*
▶ *any limitations on what you can pay in or take out*
▶ *whether you can change the plan in any way*
▶ *your cancellation rights*
▶ *how to complain.*

Suitability Report

The Suitability Report sets out why the adviser considers the product and provider they have recommended to you is suitable for your needs.

Other sources of help and advice

Your employer
Some employers will arrange financial advice surgeries where a financial adviser is available to help you with financial issues. Sometimes these include specific retirement planning seminars which will often cover many aspects of retirement as well as financial issues.

It is always worth taking advantage of these services as they can be extremely beneficial, especially if your employer is contributing to the cost. However, just because they are being provided by your employer don't ignore the advice on finding and using an adviser covered earlier in this chapter.

Insight
We provide an employee advice service for a number of employers where we regularly visit the employers' premises and provide advice 'surgeries' for staff. This works well for the member of staff, the employer and us. The member of staff can talk to someone they know and trust and the employer is seen to be providing a valued benefit for their staff.

Citizens' Advice Bureau
Whilst not specifically giving advice on retirement issues, the Citizens' Advice Bureau (CAB) can be extremely helpful with issues such as state benefits. It is always worth consulting them at retirement about any benefits you may be entitled to, particularly pension credits.

The government
Believe it or not the government can be a good source of factual information about retirement, particularly with regard to state pensions and benefit. As you might expect these days, most of the information is web-based and a list of helpful websites is given at the end of this book.

If you are approaching state retirement age you will be contacted by The Pension Service (which is the government department that deals with the state pension) to give you details of how much state pension you will be entitled to and ask if you want to start claiming it immediately or delay it in return for a higher pension.

The Financial Services Authority (FSA)

Whilst they cannot provide specific advice, the FSA provides information on a wide range of financial topics including several on retirement.

This service is called 'Money Made Clear' and includes:

▶ *step-by-step guides that explain money matters in plain English*
▶ *tools and calculators that help you plan*
▶ *comparison tables that compare best rates including pension annuities.*

Consumer websites

There are a number of consumer websites that offer help and advice on areas regarding money.

Also although not strictly speaking consumer websites, most Trade Associations also have websites with consumer information on them that are not linked to a particular company. For example, the Investors Managers Association (IMA) provide information on investing in Unit Trusts and OEICs, and the Stock Exchange has information on investing directly in shares and other traded investments.

Finally, there are a number of encyclopaedia websites that explain in factual terms types of investment.

Insight

All types of websites have their limitations. Pure consumer websites often have blogs where people can state their views and these may be coloured by their personal experiences,

(Contd)

either good or bad. Trade Association websites' primary purpose is to promote their members' products, and encyclopaedia websites are often unedited. As always in this situation, the best thing to do is collect as much information as possible and do not rely on any one source.

Commercial websites

There are a vast number of commercial websites that can be a valuable source of information although they can be difficult to distinguish from consumer sites and, as so often with the web, separating the wheat from the chaff is not always that easy.

Broadly speaking commercial websites can be divided into two categories:

▶ *those run by specific financial services companies*
▶ *comparison sites.*

Those run by specific financial services companies will promote the products and services of the company in question, but may also contain useful generic information.

Comparison websites will list products and services offered by a number of different companies. The most well known examples of comparison sites are those that advertise motor insurance on television. They can be extremely useful for sourcing the best priced product, but you have to be careful that you are comparing like for like.

For example, the highest interest rate listed for a deposit account may not be catch free, there may be penalties for withdrawals, a requirement to take out another product or the rate may only be on offer for a short period.

The other point to note about these sites is that they will often have a link for you to receive further advice. These will nearly always link to a commercial company that has paid the comparison site to be linked in this way.

Newspapers and magazines

Most newspapers regularly run articles on specific financial issues and have associated websites where you can look up previous articles.

Of particular note is that many newspapers publish tables of deposit interest rates which can be extremely helpful in finding the best rate.

TEN POINTS TO REMEMBER

1 *Independent advisers act for you, have to find the most suitable product for you and in most circumstances have to give you the option of paying by a fee.*

2 *Tied advisers act for the company they represent and will usually take commission if they arrange a product for you.*

3 *Check the level of qualifications an adviser holds and also ask for their experience in dealing with the issue you require advice on.*

4 *When dealing with a financial adviser expect them:*
  ▷ *to be open and honest about how much and in what form they get paid*
  ▷ *to spend time finding out about your requirements*
  ▷ *to point out the disadvantages as well as the advantages of what they are recommending.*

5 *Commission can be a convenient way to pay for financial advice but:*
  ▷ *it is not free*
  ▷ *the adviser may only get paid if you buy something.*

6 *Make sure you understand what is being suggested before signing on the dotted line.*

7 *When you first meet the adviser you should be given a Services and Cost Disclosure that sets out how they do business and how they get paid.*

8 *Before signing up to a product you should be given a Key Features Document that explains how the product works.*

9 *Shortly before or just after your have taken out a product you should be given a Suitability Report explaining why the adviser considers the product right for you.*

10 *Other sources of information can include:*
- ▷ *your employer*
- ▷ *Citizens' Advice*
- ▷ *the FSA*
- ▷ *consumer websites*
- ▷ *newspapers and magazines.*

Further help

Government websites

The Pension Service: www.thepensionservice.gov.uk

The Directgov website contains a lot of detail on the state pension and other state benefits and can be found at www.direct.gov.uk

The Financial Services Authority (FSA): http://www.moneymadeclear.fsa.gov.uk/

The Pension Advisory Service: www.pensionsadvisoryservice.org.uk

---

Consumer websites

www.moneysavingexpert.com
www.fool.co.uk/
www.thisismoney.co.uk
www.investopedia.com
www.trustnet.com
www.iii.co.uk/funds
www.morningstar.co.uk

Comparison websites

www.moneysupermarket.com
www.gocompare.com/money

Trade Association websites

Investment Managers Association – advice on investing in Unit Trusts and OEICs:
www.investmentuk.org/investors

Association of British Insurers – advice on life insurance and pensions:
www.abi.org.uk/Information/Consumers

State pension

For information on the state pension including obtaining a pension forecast contact:

State Pension Forecasting Team
Future Pension Centre
Tyneview Park
Whitley Road
Newcastle upon Tyne
NE98 1BA
Telephone: 0845 3000 168

https://secure.thepensionservice.gov.uk/statepensionforecast/

To trace details of missing accounts

For National Savings, bank and building society accounts, go to:
www.mylostaccount.org.uk

If you prefer to deal by phone or post you will need to contact the following organizations individually:

Lost Accounts Manager
The British Bankers' Association
Pinners Hall
105–8 Old Broad Street
London EC2N 1EX
Telephone: 020 7216 8909

Lost Savings
The Building Societies Association
6th Floor, York House
23 Kingsway
London WC2B 6UJ
Telephone: 020 7520 5900

National Savings and Investments
Tracing Service
Blackpool FY3 9YP
Telephone: 0845 964 5000

Pension Tracing Service
The Pension Service
Tyneview Park
Whitley Road,
Newcastle Upon Tyne
NE98 1BA
Telephone: 0845 6002 537

Also for pensions, enter 'Pensions Tracing' into a search engine,
or go to:
https://secureonline.dwp.gov.uk/tps-directgov/en/contact-tps/
pension-tracing-form.asp

For many other types of savings and investments try the Unclaimed
Assets Register at www.uar.co.uk.

Unclaimed Assets Register
PO Box 9501
Nottingham
NG80 1WD
Telephone: 0870 241 1713

Obtaining an exemption certificate

You can get details on obtaining an Age Exemption Certificate by writing to:

HM Revenue and Customs
National Insurance Contributions Office
Contributor Caseworker
Longbenton
Newcastle upon Tyne
NE98 1ZZ

Alternatively call the National Insurance Contributions helpline: 0845 302 1479

Index

Reference should also be made to five-minute jargon buster on pages xii–xvii